A gift
of knowledge
for
understanding
the purpose
of life

Into Eternity

The Nature of the Universe
and Your Contribution to It

channeled
information
revealed through
Tom Fitzgerald

and edited by
JeanAnn Fitzgerald

Published by
The Energy Circuit, Inc.
Reno, Nevada

e-mail: eci@marcus.reno.nv.us

web site: http://www.energycircuit.com

Copyright © 1993, © 1998
by Thomas C. Fitzgerald and JeanAnn Fitzgerald
All rights reserved.

No part of this book may be reproduced or transmitted in any form or by any means, electronic or mechanical, including photocopying, recording, or by any information storage and retrieval system, without permission in writing from the publisher.

Cover and illustrations by JeanAnn Fitzgerald

Printed in the United States of America

First Edition
April 1993

Second Edition
January 1998

ISBN 0-9662133-0-0

Other books published by The Energy Circuit:

Angelheart, A Metaphysical Story of Love

About the spirit Marcus who presents this information

Marcus

The greaterbeings, your higher selves, have asked me to speak for them and in so doing be of service to you.

My own experience at being human is heavily concentrated in the Greek and Roman times. That's important because you need a tie. It doesn't mean I've not had other lives, I've just had very intense experiences during the Greek and Roman heydays.

There was a lot of good weather during those years and humans got healthy because of it. There was general peace due to a lull in the massive human slaughtering that had occurred up to then. It was fun for us to come in and be human, and then go out again. The life spans were not overly long, 40-50 years or so. It was easy to be a child and die, to be a mother, a father, a soldier and a slave. It was easy to be a dictator, or to be somebody thinking up the idea of what you would call democracy. It was a good time as there was a lot to be learned. It was fun.

But humans forgot about all this so that by 900 A.D. it was horrible again. Of course the weather patterns had changed too. People got away from the sun and its energy. They looked more inward in a negative way instead of outward in a positive way, and that's why we had the Dark Ages.

But who and where we've been in my greaterbeing's incarnations is less important than where you humans are going with the information I am passing on to you. With this information we can all proceed effectively into the limitless possibilities of eternity.

Subject Listing

	Page
Prologue	1
Chapter 1 Sharing the Concepts	3
Explanation of Terms	5
Chapter 2 Energy	11
Basic Fabric of the Universe	13
Auras	14
Energy circuit	16
Characteristics	18
It is not love	20
How to multiply	21
Sharing	22
More than enough	23
Too much?	23
With creatures and plants	24
High energy conditions	26
Residual energy	27
For everything and everyone	29
Negative = low	30
Bedeviling forms	32
Always positive	33
Chapter 3 Innerbeing	35
That Soul Inside You	37
It's just there	38
You can't see it	38
Humans are essential	39
From the greaterbeing	39

Chapter 3 *continued*
    Free will and the lifeplan 42
    Free will vs. lifeplan 44
    Greaterbeing-brain connection 47
    Conscious mind 50
    Subconscious mind 51
    Dreaming 52
    Superconscious 55
    Choosing the human 56
    Everyone has one 58
    Time of entry 59
    Astral projection 59
    Walk-ins 61
    Animal energy forms 63
    Purposes of animals 63
    Animals amongst us 66
    Passing over 68

Chapter 4 **The Middleground** 73
    Between Spirit and Human 75
    Purpose of physical guardians 76
    Physical guardian origination 78
    Forgotten physical guardians 79
    Helper spirits 82
    Human ingenuity 83
    Innerbeings in transit 84
    Why innerbeings are there 84
    Holidays heighten awareness 89
    Available for assistance 90
    Spiritual instructors 92

SUBJECT LISTING

```
          Time for anything . . . . . . . . . . . . . .93
          High jinks  . . . . . . . . . . . . . . . . . .93
          Human vs. greaterbeing tie  . . . . . .98
          Animals . . . . . . . . . . . . . . . . . . . .99
```

Chapter 5 Greaterbeings 101
          Your Higher Self 103
          There is only what is 104
          Awareness of being 105
          Activity is cerebral 105
          Cooperation 107
          Endeavors 109
          Reincarnation 111
          Sum total of experiences 114
          Here for a lifeplan 116
          Benefits from reincarnation 121
          Breaking past life ties 122
          Reliving the past 123
          Greaterbeing to human tap-in 125
          Sifting through information 127
          Maturation 128

Chapter 6 Tribulations 131
          Life Can Be Difficult 133
          Human condition 133
          Pacts for experience 135
          Disease .136
          Human commonality 137
          All experience is positive 138
          Karma 139
          Lifeplan interference 140
          We travel together 142

    Future level 144
    Mental-to-mental 144

Chapter 8 The Ultimate Source 147
   God and Us 149
    Ultimate Source begins eternity 149
    Ultimate Source replicates 150
    Creating the cosmos 151
    Creativity was not enough 152
    Solution is physical 153
    Sharing without regeneration 154
    Regeneration now building 155
    Ultimate Being shares with all 156

We Love to Communicate 159

Epilogue 161

You Are, And Therefore I Love You 166

Channeler's Comments 169

About the Channeler 178

About the Editor .179

Prologue

By Tom Fitzgerald

It is hard to imagine life without a true friend such as Marcus. Our greaterbeings have shared many lives and so there is a definite comfort level between Marcus and myself. We share many stories about times past; our adventures have been fun and fulfilling.

Marcus of course sounds like me because he uses my body to speak through. But his word phrasing, sentence structure, the way he holds my body and hands, the way he sits straight up in a chair--all are different mannerisms from my own. He has spoken through me so many times now that I know his presence very well.

Communication between just the two of us can be described as a presentation of pictures. It's right there. We both see the exact same thing. Since we see the same thing simultaneously, the communication is finished. It's instantaneous. There's no need for interpretation as there's no difference between our perceptions. There's no concern about 'was the thought properly transmitted?' If everyone on Earth today could communicate the way Marcus and I do, there wouldn't be a need for talking to each other. It would be a very quiet planet. Talking is fine as far as it goes, it is the present way humans pass on a concept from one to the other.

In my classes and seminars people always asked "Who do you channel?" I would explain to them that

I channel a consortium of greaterbeings who wish to give information to our side. And then they would say, "Yes, but what is the name?"

Because so many expect a singular name, someone to identify with, we asked the greaterbeings who would be the spokesperson. "Marcus will do the talking for us."

Marcus is not interested in becoming a celebrity. He is very interested in getting this information across to people so they will better understand their relationship to the spiritual side. He is a cheerleader for getting people to learn as much about spirituality as quickly as possible. He shares the enthusiasm JeanAnn and I have for helping people learn and grow and understand the metaphysical side of life.

I am thrilled that Marcus speaks through me. I invite all of you to share the joy and wisdom he brings into our lives.

Reno, Nevada
Winter, 1997

P.S. Other than rewording some sentences for clarity, this edition has a terminology change in that "entity" is replaced with the word greaterbeing. The meaning of the term "entity" is too broad, so the new word was deemed more precise. The resulting relationship between greaterbeing and innerbeing is quite nice.

Sharing the Concepts

Marcus

When we first came through to talk with Tom and JeanAnn, we used words that were new not only to them, but to the others in the group as well. (We came through in English--we could have come through in another language but that would have made no sense to anybody in the room!) The reason we chose the words that we did was so there would be no misunderstanding about what we were trying to pass through to you the reader.

When you read our definition you will say, "Oh, they must mean...." Yes, we do. But the reason those other words aren't in the book or in this chapter on definitions, is because there are too many variations of what they mean. We are interested in focusing your attention on a commonality that can be shared with everyone. Thus we have used the words that now follow.

1
Explanation of Terms

Astral projection - An event transpiring usually during sleep or relaxation in which the innerbeing (soul) stretches itself out from the body to visit and communicate with other places/people on earth or beyond. The innerbeing is not disconnected from its body during this event, it is merely extended from it.

Aura - That band of energy surrounding the surface of any energy producing object, especially the human body; may contain one or more colors.

Channeling - The passing of information from the spiritual side to human beings. Psychic readings are typically done during conscious channeling, i.e. the channeler hears/sees the information and passes it on while in a conscious state. Trance channeling refers to information presentation by a spirit through an unconscious person.

Conscious mind - That active part of the innerbeing housed in the brain which interprets only part of the messages transmitted from the physical senses; that part which makes logical decisions.

Energy - That force initiated and supplied by the Ultimate Source; the basic fabric of the universe; is regenerated and multiplied by all that has been created; synonymous with eternal love.

Greaterbeing - One of an exponential group of on-going spiritual entities that is eternal from its point of creation forward; with The Ultimate Source they are co-creators of the cosmos in order to enrich the experience and energy levels of themselves and The Ultimate Source; a greaterbeing projects part of itself (an innerbeing) into a human so as to mature from that human's experience and energy generation; synonymous with spiritual entity.

Eternity - Beginning from when The Ultimate Source became aware of its own existence, and extending into the future never ending.

God - See Ultimate Source.

Helper Spirit - An innerbeing in the middleground with vast experience with which to aid humans in their everyday lives; can be projected into the middlezone directly from the greaterbeing; can be an innerbeing whose earthly life has ended but chooses the middleground in order to assist humans still on earth.

Human condition - The state of physical, spiritual, mental and social situations at a given period in human history.

EXPLANATION OF TERMS

Innerbeing - That part of a greaterbeing projected from itself into a human body or into the middleground as a helper or instructor for example; the life-giving force in every human body; the human innerbeing's personality is determined by the greaterbeing's desire to learn certain life lessons, and selected experiences from past incarnations; this personality is imbedded in the innerbeing's conscious, subconscious and superconscious to determines the human's reactions within that life; also see Soul.

Instructor - An innerbeing in the middleground that is able to help other middleground innerbeings and earthly humans learn about the plan for eternity; can be an innerbeing not yet returned to the greaterbeing, or a spirit specially sent into the middleground for that purpose by its spiritual entity.

Intuition - A reception by the human mind not based on the five physical senses; information or suggestions from the spiritual side into the consciousness via the subconscious and superconscious; see Psychic experience.

Lifeplan - A set of life goals laid out by a greaterbeing prior to infusing a human body with a soul; a blue-print for the life that the human will generally follow in its journey; includes lessons and/or challenges for the greaterbeing's development; its purpose is to enable the greaterbeing to learn what it has desired.

Mental-to-mental - The ability to communicate concepts from one being to another without the use of vocalizing words or reading; the communication form used on the spiritual side; also known as brain-to-brain.

Middleground - That quasi-physical area between the physical earth and the spiritual side; comprised of the gray area closest to humans, and the whiter area nearer the greaterbeings; populated by instructors, helpers, guardians and lost souls among other spiritual beings; synonymous with middlerange and middlezone.

Near-death experience - A situation wherein a physical body is in critical condition or has ceased to function; during this time the innerbeing reaches over to the spiritual side in an attempt to return there, but is instructed to return to its body and continue its life.

Other side - That which is not physical; the spiritual realm.

Physical guardian - The single spirit assigned to an innerbeing at birth which remains the human's lifetime; is responsible for protection of the physical body so that there is time enough for the innerbeing to complete the lifeplan; additional physical guardians come and go as needed throughout that life.

Psychic experience - A situation wherein the

human mind perceives something without using the five physical senses.

Psychic interpreter - A human being with the past and present experiences enabling him/her to act as the channel through which greaterbeings can pass information to humans concerning the plan for eternity.

Psychic medium - A human being who acts as the channel through which innerbeings and instructors in the middleground can communicate with humans.

Reincarnation - The process whereby a greaterbeing repeatedly provides human bodies with part of itself in order to achieve further maturation and also share in the energy feed-back from the human side.

Soul - That spiritual aspect of a human which does not die with the body, but instead returns to its spiritual greaterbeing; synonymous with innerbeing.

Spirit - That part of a greaterbeing projected into the middleground as a guardian, an instructor, a helper, or a human innerbeing which has not returned to its greaterbeing; used loosely when referring to greaterbeings also.

Subconscious - That part of the innerbeing which is always active and can interpret all messages from the physical senses; can make instantaneous decisions based on the total input from the environment past and present; also receives input through the superconscious from the spiritual greaterbeing.

Suffering - A necessary tribulation for humanity; will benefit humankind by enabling the greaterbeings to mature and become well-rounded in their experience and thereby move beyond the point of suffering.

Superconscious - That passive part of the innerbeing which acts as a translator between the greaterbeing and the human; is also used for information storage.

Tapping in - Becoming connected to the spiritual side so that communication can occur.

Trance - A relaxed state of the human consciousness; during this time the subconscious also steps aside so another innerbeing or greaterbeing can temporarily enter through the superconscious and use that body for verbal communication with humans; also called channeling.

Ultimate Source - The Original Being in our universe from whom other forms and energies initially commenced; in conjunction with greaterbeings and humans, creates the future of the universe; synonymous with God, The Ultimate Being, The Original Source, etc.

Energy

Marcus

Energy is the basic foundation of the entire existence--our side, your side, all sides.

It is not easy to define in your words because it is unfortunately, a word that has many meanings. Energy as we refer to it in this book is the consummate, universal feeling shared by humans and their creators on our side. It is this sharing that goes on and grows for eternity, will never end, will never be less than it currently is, will always be more in the future. It will carry us beyond anything the mind is capable of imagining. It is a feeling, a being, an existence that everybody should focus on at all times.

2
Basic Fabric of the Universe

Imagine that you are wearing a newly-developed pair of eyeglasses that are psychically-sensitive spectacles. These special glasses enable you to see the effervescent energy emitted by the human body. Then imagine you are in a shopping mall watching people through your magical glasses as they walk from store to store. Through these glasses you are able to see each footprint left on the pavement by their energy overflow.

Energy like this tends to slough off constantly from every human being. It's like walking across the room without drying off after a shower--the water from your body would drop off until it was all gone. You only have a finite amount of water clinging to your body after a shower, but your body is always creating energy. So your residual energy fallout would be like stepping from a shower and walking away with the water falling off for the rest of your life! This residue can be thought of as a psychic fingerprint. Unlike the water, it requires much more time for this energy print to evaporate. In actuality, all living bodies leave energy residue like this on the things they contact.

Auras

The body produces energy primarily for the purpose of conducting its living. It also transmits some energy into the environment, and some remains in close proximity to the body. People are able to see this energy around the body and it has been named the aura. This aura is the same energy glow that you would get off of any energy source anywhere in the world such as a power plant, water falling, or an engine giving off heat. It's all the same type of thing.

For some, learning to see auras is difficult. Normally you look with your conscious minds to perceive things. But the **sub**conscious mind recognizes psychic things such as auras more easily. When people accidentally see an aura, it is because their subconscious is active at the time. Upon noticing the aura, humans generally look directly at it, and suddenly it is nowhere to be seen. This is because this direct focus is done with the conscious mind.

In looking for auras, remember that the point whereon the eyes focus is transmitted to the conscious mind, and that which is in the peripheral vision is registered in the subconscious. Although the aura can be seen around the edges of the body, don't look there to see it. In doing this, you'll be using your conscious mind which has more difficulty seeing them.

Instead look at the bridge of a person's nose with your eyes relaxed. By concentrating on that point, the edge of their head will be in your peripheral vision. Now you are then looking with your subconscious and should be able to see the aura. Once you are able to see auras regularly in this manner, the logical transition is for the conscious mind to perceive them also. Then you will be able to consistently look for people's auras and have success.

The aura may appear as a one to two inch wide clear translucent band around a person's body. The band might look just a little darker or brighter than the background. Others see auras as a band of one color, or as a combination of colors.

A positive aura is brighter or more intensely colored. It has clarity and it is wide. There are certain colors that are never bright or intense; they're just there. An emerald green is not the same as a chocolate brown. The brown will always carry a dullness to it and the emerald green will be more intense, brighter, clearer, and seem more positive.

The width of the band denotes how much that person is in tune with the spiritual side. The spiritual side contributes energy to the human's energy. The combined energies result in *even more energy than just the combination.* It is not the result of simply adding 2 + 2, but more like 2 x 2. Because energy is dynamic, when it is combined the result is greater than just the combination of the original two factors. Thus the aura band can be wider when the spiritual element is added. This combination is like having a full electrical charge.

White (not clear, but a brilliant white) is seldom seen because it signifies a great tie-in with the other side. Spiritual tie-ins range from the brilliant white into more of the gold. A pale yellow connotes that the bright gold is being drained down into a brown color.

Brown, although associated with the earth from

which things grow, has also come to signify waste from the human body. If an aura has a brown spot in it, the significance is usually of an injury or illness.

The grays approach the black color. Black is deadly, almost death, and many times is death. Black signifies the close-down of a life. There will not be a shiny black unless it is the final burst of energy before that individual's death.

Colors do not really carry the significance some have assigned to them: "This one is spiritual, this color is positive and forward-looking, and this one isn't". The color is more an interpretation by the person wearing it. A person's aura is much like the color of clothing worn that day. Sometimes what we see is their favorite color, it's just *their color*.

What if you see a golden aura with some greens and blues in it? It is the happiness of that person coming out in their colors. If you see an individual with a bright lime green color about them and it is big and brilliant and that person is happy, share the joy because there is nothing wrong. That individual has just found a way to overcome the energy level; instead of reflecting the golden energy, they want *their color* reflected.

This book begins with the topic of energy because it is the basis for everything in creation; energy is the basic building block of the universe. Whether it be animal, vegetable, mineral or spiritual, everything is made from energy.

Energy circuit

A diagram of the energy circuit is basically a hor-

izontal figure eight. It is a continuous form having no beginning and no end. This figure eight is used as the symbol for eternity since it has no beginning or ending. Energy originates from The Ultimate Source and is an expression of Its love for creation. So this figure eight has also become a symbol of eternal love, unconditional love. The Original Being shares with us this unconditional love with no strings attached. It is a symbol recognized throughout the universe. This is why it is usually the first greeting formed by middleground spirits who communicate through automatic writing.

The human body is a link in this grand circuit of spiritual and physical energy that is shared and revitalized by each participant of the loop. The Ultimate Source originated the energy flow from Itself to the spiritual beings It created. These spiritual beings added to the circuit by creating innerbeings (souls) which are the life forces behind human bodies. Mankind takes the energy, revitalizes it and sends it back into the spiritual circuit. It is a two-way circuit which multiplies the available energy because of each participant.

Humans would cease to exist without this energy flow. The Ultimate Source and greaterbeings would not cease to exist without the human energy component. But without a human energy contribution they just wouldn't grow as easily to the level of which they are capable.

Characteristics

It is the nature of energy to be interactive; it is not static and is always moving. All energy is the same whether it be spiritual, physical, creative, or whatever. Rather than being descriptive terms, these are actually purposes for which to use energy. Energy is much like water that can be used to bathe yourself, nurture houseplants, or generate hydroelectric power. It is all the same water used for various purposes. And likewise all energy is the same thing, but is utilized to achieve an infinite number of desired results.

Physical energy runs the human body and controls everything about it. It is greater than any other energy on earth. This energy supply is greater than what it takes to run human bodies, so there is always an excess of it. This extra energy can be likened to lava spewed out by a volcano. But the volcano erupts only occasionally, whereas the body is throwing off energy **all** of the time. This energy, or unconditional love, is created by a combination of the spiritual greaterbeing and the human body. It is the greaterbeing who initially infuses this life energy into the body. The ingestion/digestion processes of the body plus the sleeping and caring for itself adds to the energy and helps it to multiply. The combination of spiritual and physical creates more energy than needed to keep the body going.

As long as the human being is alive, there will be a tap into the greaterbeing's energy. This results in a double-flow and merging. The result is an energy stronger than either the greaterbeing's or the human's energy alone. Each human acts like an electrical substation receiving energy, revitalizing it, and whipping it back out at a higher level. If even more energy is received from the greaterbeing, the body can be even healthier. In an optimum state the body is able to produce more energy for itself, and for the greaterbeing in return. And of course when there is an abundance of energy, there is much more to be shared with other humans.

Energy is always flowing. It is around everyone and it is always there. You never run out of energy and you have more of it than you need, so it can always be shared. In fact, it multiplies when shared with others. You do not pass life-sustaining energy, just the excess. Because of who you are, you constantly draw from the sources and pass it on to others. Since this energy flows naturally out of the human body, when two people are together there is more excess energy. When there are three or four or more people adding to the energy pool, it multiplies exponentially.

Even those people who think they don't have enough energy to get through their days still have an excess of it. Let us say for example, that we're holding hands and you are really on your last ounce of steam. Because your energy is below normal, you might be taking it in through your right hand at a low level, but on your left it's flowing out at a much higher speed. As it passes through you, your body energy jumps up immensely, and at the same time whips it on through to others. Your body and your greaterbeing together have the ability to do this. The simple act of taking the energy in and passing it back out whips it up to a stronger level.

If you tap into others, you can not drain them completely because you will receive only their excess energy. When you are feeling tired and/or depressed, it is usually unproductive to withdraw from others. The easiest way to revitalize yourself is not by seeking a solitary state, but rather by placing yourself in a large group of people! Energy passes easily from one to the other when people are together. In no time at all, your batteries will be recharged with the excess energy from the others.

It is not love

Energy has nothing to do with traditional ideas of love. Some people only associate love within their particular family. Many people equate love to a specific individual or an animal. Some have actually taken love to mean feelings towards an inanimate object. "Love" is such a broad generalization that it gets away from what energy really is.

If someone announces, "I don't feel good today, I have a cold, I just feel awful," people nearby can respond in a helpful manner. "We can make you feel better! You stand in the middle of us and we'll all hold hands around you. The accelerated energy we pass on to you will zap you so much that you'll feel better whether you want to or not."

This energy transference has nothing to do with love. If the people in the group thought they were passing love to the sick individual, there could be somebody standing in that group saying "**I do not love** that person!" In so doing that one person would block the energy flow almost entirely.

How to multiply

Energy shared between people tends to be positive. For example, if you don't have much energy or feel negative and down-hearted, you can cheer up when somebody comes along who's really happy. What you do is take excess energy from the other person to fill in the valleys of your own energy level. By combining energies like this everybody feels better. It is a pleasurable feeling to share energy.

Sometimes a group of people will get together, and as a result everyone feels really great and actually kind of high. Their excess energy has been shared so that everybody benefits. In a group (the larger the better) each one can feel really good by sharing energy. Even if one doesn't have a lot of excess energy to give, the combined effect still makes everyone feel better.

Once people get together on a continual basis for the purpose of sharing and making each other feel better, everyone's going to learn how to share energy. They're going to look forward to it and it is going to be a positive situation of eternal and unconditional love.

An example of shared positive energy is the joining of hands at the dinner table before eating. If some diners are new to this practice, their first thought might be, "What kind of weird religious thing is this anyhow?" The host or hostess might say, "Let's just share the energy and feel good. Let's look into each others eyes and wish us all well." The new-comers will brighten up. "Wow! There are no strings attached to this! I don't have to hear a prayer I don't want to hear, I don't have to say a prayer I don't want to say. We're just going to feel good because of each other. I can handle that!" All of a sudden everyone is being flooded with goodness--how can anyone complain? Right away all will feel good, smile at each other and be pleased at being together.

Sharing

Energy is a gift to all mankind from the Ultimate Source and so must be spread to those outside of one's group. No matter the size of your group, limiting your energy to just that segment of the population is contrary to the whole intent. Energy is to be shared in order to make **everyone** feel good. When everyone feels good there is even more energy to be shared. It is a self-propelling upward spiral.

Socially acceptable hand-holding by strangers and acquaintances before a meal is an excellent way for people to learn how to share energy. Through physical contact, everyone can easily feel the flow and know it's happening. Sharing is not just for people you know and like; we should even share it with total strangers.

Strangers are not likely to accept a hug or let you hold their hand, but once you know what energy flow feels like, sharing becomes easier to do without even touching the receiver. This can be practiced by mentally wishing the other person well. Or you can visualize in your mind that you are physically hugging them. Or imagine that a feeling of happiness is flowing like electricity from you to the other person.

These strangers are those who serve you in restaurants, the person in the car next to you at the traffic light, the people in the house across the street. All of them can benefit from your excess energy. Everyone should be more aware of the energy they have and dispense it to others, because it is there to be used.

Energy can be sent very easily while talking on the telephone because of the way voices are transmitted through the telephone lines. The energy will flow right to the person at the other end. They will almost feel the telephone itself glow; in return they will glow with the receipt.

More than enough

You never run out of energy and always have more than you need. Sharing is **not** like passing on life-sustaining energy of which you only have a finite amount so when it's gone you're dead. Energy is not finite because we are constantly drawing from the infinite sources and passing it around. There is no need to be stingy with energy. It's not like money that grows when stashed away in a bank account. Energy grows especially well when it is invested in others.

Too much?

Since all living things have a built-in protection system against receiving too much energy, no one has ever suffered from overexposure. You can get to the point where you really feel the energy and maybe think it's too much, but you can't get dangerously **over**-energized because the extra is just sloughed off. Remember the analogy of excess energy dripping off the body like water after a shower? When you receive too much energy, you just slough off more of it. Every person has only a certain capacity. You can't put twelve ounces of water into an eight ounce container because it just runs over the sides. It isn't going to work with you either, you have only a certain capacity. Most people run from a little bit low to significantly below their capacity. If you are at your capacity, you will just pass the overflow onto other people who need it to raise their own levels.

With creatures and plants

Other living creatures and plant life also contribute energy to the planet at a sub-energy level. This sub-energy is entirely necessary to keep the earth going and is very critical to it.

As with all energy, there is an interplay, an interaction of all this energy from humans, animals, and objects. You can give energy to the plants and animals and fish and other living creatures, and they can give it back in return. There is an on-going symbiotic relationship wherein they can give humans energy and mankind can share with them. When humans are sharing energy with other life forms, their energy gets caught up and can go to the spiritual side along with the human energy. But it is not a necessary thing that their energy be included, it just happens.

You can share energy with other living things because you desire to. People have experienced phenomenal plant growth, or have caused animals to be sustained when they probably should have died. People cause these events to occur because they are free and open with the sharing of their energy. Scientific experiments have been done for a long time with mean-spirited people approaching plants with murderous intent and discovering that the plants can "shriek" and fall limp because they feel threatened. This happens because lesser life forms are able to sense a lot from humans.

Plants and animals are especially receptive to those humans who emit no threatening energy. (Small children who still function at a psychic level can also sense this in the same way the animals and plants do.) So these lesser life forms do take some energy from us and can use it, and you in turn can integrate theirs with yours. But it is still a dual-level energy form: theirs is required for the earth, whereas yours is required to keep in touch with the spiritual side.

Most people have been unconsciously utilizing this energy exchange between life forms. Why is it that people take flowers and plants to the sick and those in hospitals? It is not just that they look and smell good. There's an energy given off of them, there's a life force that's there to be shared. Many times when people are hospitalized their conscious level is weakened to the point that their subconscious is dominant. More in tune with their subconscious, sick people can therefore more readily sense the earth's natural energies.

Another successful experiment has been animals visiting the elderly. The animal usually gives off a non-threatening form of energy which the elderly readily take in. The elderly persons then feel willing to pass the energy back to the animals. The animals, like humans and plant life, cannot be over-energized because everything has a built-in protection system to prevent that from happening.

High energy conditions

Some individuals find it easy to pass energy on to others. You probably know some of these people--they're the ones who make you feel good just by being in their company. These people are more attuned to who they are and are more at ease with who they happen to be. They are able to freely utilize their energies for themselves, and therefore find it a simple matter to also pass it along to others (even though they may not realize they do it).

Fortunate individuals may be far enough along in their life lessons to have even more extra energy to pass around. They have already learned at least the majority of their lessons, so they are more at rest with themselves, they are more at ease. Because they are not struggling with life's lessons, they have plenty of excess energy to share with those around them.

Higher energy also exists when the body is healthy. In this state it is better able, in conjunction with the greaterbeing, to generate more excess energy to spread around.

Another high energy situation can exist just by being aware of the energy and what can be done with it. Realizing that you can do something raises your confidence in being successful. A positive attitude brings positive results. It works the same way on the metaphysical level. You already know that a kind word, a warm smile or a hug can work wonders. When you can't do that in person, mentally send some extra energy to the grouchy store clerk who would be insulted by a physical hug, but who may not be aware of receiving a psychic embrace. Or you can zap out some extra mental energy to your child at school who is struggling with a math test at that moment. The possibilities of sharing become endless.

Because we normally receive energy from our greaterbeing, it is a simple matter to request even more when you need it. Give your greaterbeing a mental hug in order to experience a revitalization of yourself.

One can practice throwing out energy to total strangers--those people standing in line with you or those whom you pass on the street. Everyone should be more aware of the energy they have and that it can be thrown out to others. This should be done constantly because it's there for that purpose. This conscious sharing of energy and learning to utilize it acts as an initializer for further metaphysical development.

Residual energy

Everywhere human beings go they leave a residual trace of themselves, excess energy that sloughs off like dripping water. It can be recognized by others in much the same way a dog or cat smells out a territory to determine which animals have been there before it. This excess human energy is recognized by the human's superconscious.

You can walk into a strange house and feel very uncomfortable for no explainable reason. This can be due to your superconscious' recognition of unsettling residual energy left behind by previous residents. Perhaps those family members fought a lot and were very unhappy. Maybe an important change occurred in their lives while living there.

While walking through the remains of a long ago town one can ascertain the overall mood of the residents--whether they were boisterous, industrious or serious as a group. (Of course the same can be done with any functioning town or area.) If there were a particularly strong person in the community it is possible to "read" the residual energy which that individual left behind in its particular area. Perhaps that person was especially happy living there, wanted to control the other residents, was a lonely child growing up, or whatever the case might have been.

Likewise, objects from another person's life can be psychically read by holding the object and opening yourself up to the kind of person who owned it. A woodcarver's knife might present a mental picture of the great love he had in creating his works. You might feel the wood itself, or the pride he had in finishing the piece. The smoothness of a lucky pebble once belonging to a gambler in times past might create mental images of a swarthy-complexioned gent with pitch-dark hair and moustache who never went anywhere without his lucky black hat.

These energy fingerprints that everyone leaves behind will ultimately fade because they are no longer connected to a human body to replenish that energy. Metaphysically sensitive people are able to read these fingerprints on objects centuries after they were left there.

The amount of energy transferred to an object depends upon the magnitude of the person's energy overflow. If a person exudes a lot of energy, it will take longer for the fingerprint to dissipate. The handler's attitude also affects the amount of energy transferred. If an object is merely a thing in the person's environment, there will be little transferred to it. If a person is very fond of an object, there will be more energy left on it.

For everything and everyone

There is no such thing as wasting energy in non-productive ways. **All human endeavors are proper learning experiences.** However the human decides to use the energy is correct since the greater-being always gains from any experience.

For example, it is a human judgment that hating others is a waste of energy. Humans who move into the hate arena will learn because of others' reactions to their hate. They will also learn the reactions from other humans who support that hate. They and their greaterbeings will learn--perhaps not in this life but maybe in the next--the results of that hate. If they go through the hate cycle in the here and now, in the next life perhaps they will be hated. In this case there would be a balancing, an awakening, a bottom-lining, a zeroing-out. All of this is valuable experience.

Telling people to cease hating, to stop teaching

their children to hate, may get some people's attention. For the others, surrounding them with energy and giving them a definite example to follow will be a far more positive lesson for them.

Negative = low

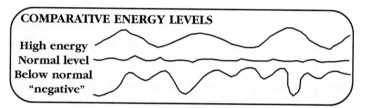

Humans speak about negative people and negative energy. To clarify this negativity, imagine a line with shallow dips or low spots. A normal amount of energy would appear as a straight line at a higher level. And of course a highly energized level would be above those two. If there are three or four below-level dips in a low-energy person, this is not a negative person or negative energy, but just *not enough* energy.

Being low on energy feels uncomfortable. People who don't feel at their best, whether emotionally, physically or intellectually, are running at an energy level below the norm. Instead of their energy level remaining at or above par, theirs never reach those levels. Sharing energy with them helps fill in the gaps so that their level rises up to normal.

When a person remains at a sub-par level, they tend to steal energy from others and are often gluttons about it. This is especially noticed when a person is taking copious amounts of energy from you much as a sick person would, or a person who you would say had a negative attitude. When the donor is metaphysically astute, they feel their energy being siphoned into that low-level glutton. You call this feeling of being pilfered a negative energy flow, and the robber a negative person because of it. But energy itself is never negative; only the absence of it is what can be termed negative.

Some people low on energy might not want any more of it. They might consciously reject it, or throw it off because they don't want to be energized. Above all, don't tell a person low on energy to plug into you because they can find a way to drain you to a level that will make you feel uncomfortable. Instead, without telling that person what you're doing, quietly plug into them with your mind. Allow your energy to go to them, and they won't know where the energy is coming from. If you revitalize them without their knowledge, you have a greater chance of succeeding.

Even a physical location can feel negative. Usually it was a favorite place of a person who had low energy. That person could still be there in spirit form robbing energy from any living creature that happens along.

Once you realize what's really happening when you feel a negative person or place, you can mentally stop your energy flow into any individual or spirit. You can even stop your energy's outflow into a "positive" being if you care to.

What you erroneously call negative energy is a self-creation by many people, and it too can be passed on from one human to another. These people have internal feelings almost as if the innerbeing is not in position securely inside the human body. There might be an opening, a protective cover missing, and they feel vulnerable. It is almost as if they feel a grinding of the innerbeing within the body. These people don't feel the full energy flow that they need to feel. They have a low level of energy receipt and so erroneously say it is negative.

People who have strongly felt the presence of negative energy, the presence of the devil or of many devils from hell, are totally insecure and have sensed the weaknesses in their innerbeing. If these people seek out others who are down below the norm level of energy and share their negativity, they can drag each other down even further. These below energy people allow their minds to interpret their lack of spiritual energy feelings into such things as the devil.

Bedeviling forms

The devil has troubled human beings for a long time. But there is no devil, he is a figment of man's imagination. Religion was an all-powerful force in the past, and the basis for organization in everyone's lives. To be a part of society, one had to be a member of the church in that area. However, some people did not happen to agree with the teachings of some churches and did not want to belong. If people did not participate, they would not be under church control. Of course the churches' hierarchies wanted everyone to participate in order to maintain their authority and control. So a way was devised to coerce the wayward. Weak church officials used the concept of a devil as a fear technique to force everyone into religion.

The devil is not as feared today as in the past. In

fact, there aren't that many who truly believe that there is a devil or a hell. Certainly not to the same high level of belief that was true a few hundred years ago.

The devil is definitely fading now because he's been replaced (unfortunately for humans) by governments that condone "evil". Governments practicing evil have replaced the devil's doing it. <u>There is no need to worry about dying and suffering later when governments will allow you to suffer **before** you die.</u> The devil could easily have been the Khmer Rouge in Cambodia, the KGB in Russia, the Stasi in East Germany, all manner of secret police in any other society. These are the "devils" in contemporary life. Governments use their devils for the same reason the churches did: to maintain authority and control, and thereby enhance their power.

The opposite also holds true. People who have definitely felt the presence of God are equal to those who sense the devil. These people know that God is actually right there solving their problems--yet their problems don't go away. Because their level of energy is so low, they cannot feel any of it. They have taken this below-average energy feeling and turned it around by feeling something, anything. Since they don't want to feel the devil, they assume it must be God coming to help them.

Always positive

A low or negative energy level sometimes feels disturbing or chaotic, but there's nothing "bad" about chaos. For example, you have chaos if your lawn sprinklers are running and the wind is blowing hard, because water blows everywhere you don't want it to go. This is not necessarily bad because many times the water is carried to where the sprinkler doesn't normally reach. The water is carried to dirt that even rain might not normally hit. If you haven't had rain in a long time, then what appears to be chaotic is actually good. So chaos in an energy sense is not necessarily bad. Everything about energy is positive in one way or another.

The Innerbeing

Marcus

In the previous chapter we talked about energy existing for eternity. We stated how human energy is necessary for the growth of universal energy. The innerbeing is the tie to bringing that human energy back to this side.

From the spiritual side, the setting in motion of the innerbeing is the most joyous creation we can think of. To actually make the innerbeing is not as exciting as taking that innerbeing and placing it inside the human. It is a great feeling for us to be temporarily human. It is so wonderful.

As we create the innerbeing, that innerbeing becomes an extension of us. To say "merely an extension" implies it's not important, so we don't use that phrase. The innerbeing is not like a puppet, not like sticking the hand into a glove and controlling it. It is giving part of us the total freedom, while still attached to us, to act for the benefit of eternity.

3
That Soul Inside You

The physical body's tap into the energy circuit is the innerbeing, the spiritual force that sustains every living human life. No one has ever seen an innerbeing with their eyes, nor felt one with fingertips. But if you mention "soul", everyone instinctively knows what you're talking about because they have sensed one in themselves.

You cannot really define a soul. You definitely cannot see a soul. You cannot physically pinpoint an innerbeing because it is not physical. You aren't sure if it is located in the organ called the heart, in the recesses of your brains, or if it permeates everything in your bodies.

The answer is all of these. You understand what a soul is because, quite simply, you are one. You just know, you don't have to have it explained. The one thing all humans share is your knowledge of what an innerbeing is because you all have one. If someone told you that you had a soul, you probably wouldn't be shocked. Your only surprise may be that others share the same feeling of being, and have a name for it.

If you walk into a room where one of your good friends is standing, it feels a certain way to you. Should you walk into another room a week later and find that same friend lying dead in a casket, it definitely feels differently--as though some part of that friend is missing.

It's just there

In your society you tend to look for ways to measure things with machines. Scientists have even weighed the human body before and after death to determine if the presence and absence of an innerbeing could be detected. (These experiments weren't entirely conclusive.)

As many of you on earth right now are becoming more aware of your psychic talents by sensing the Ultimate Source, being aware enough to feel those on the spiritual side, seeing auras around people's bodies, and even channeling communication from our side, why on earth would you need a machine to measure and define an innerbeing right next to you? (That would be like having a machine to detect colors which humans can already see and appreciate all by themselves. What's more, a machine can never truly experience an innerbeing either.) You are all capable of sensing souls quite well without the aid of a machine. Of course you will eventually invent that machine to measure what you've known about all along!

You can't see it

People have said that they have seen a soul, and then describe it as looking like a human body. These people have not seen an innerbeing because the soul doesn't look anything like a human form. In order to see a soul, it would have to be outside of the body, otherwise one just sees the body. It isn't like the tabloids tell it either: *Wife Sees Husband's Soul Leave Body upon Death.* What's actually seen in both of these cases is the residual energy that has a shape like the body. The innerbeing itself looks like a wisp of pure energy.

Humans are essential

During our present level of development in eternity, human bodies are necessary. Bodies provide physical energy that is converted through the greaterbeings to the Ultimate Source to sustain further growth on each level involved.

The Ultimate Source and the spiritual entities from which you spring could exist forever, but would fail to develop and mature as quickly without the human experience. If the earth were to cease to exist, they would collect their energies together to recreate another level much like yours. Planets and the human condition would reappear so that the greaterbeings could resume learning and share the energy generation that is produced in conjunction with humanity.

Your complex physical machines exist for greaterbeings to project an innerbeing into. The human body is comparatively frail and can have parts disfunction. The greaterbeings are eternal and your bodies are time-limited, so there is this conflict. But unfortunately at present this is the way you are.

From the greaterbeing

Most humans believe they are direct descendants

of God. They look at their bodies, realize they have a cognitive mind, and many believe they have something spiritual called a soul. Period. That is all there is--God there, and humans here. In reality it is more complex than that.

Somewhere far back in the history of eternity the Ultimate Source (God) created other spiritual beings like Itself. The Ultimate Source created countless peers, co-beings, or equals. Each one of them exists as a separate and unique entity, but is at the same time at one with the Ultimate Source because there is agreement on the Other Side. Individually and separately, the Ultimate Source and Its Co-Beings are all more wondrous than the descriptions normally attributed to God by humanity.

It was this group of Ultimate Beings who created physical matter. In spiritual form, they could not fully experience the physical universes they had formed, so they devised human beings to inhabit the planet Earth. (There are other life forms, but this book only concerns itself with the human connection to the Other Side.)

Each human is the creation of one particular Co-Being which can be called a greaterbeing from the human perspective. Greaterbeing A is the creator of John Jones and his innerbeing. Greaterbeing B is the creator of Sally Smith and her innerbeing, and so on. In the past Greaterbeing A may have created thousands of other humans and may create hundreds more in the future. Greaterbeing B may have experienced Earth through a hundred former people, and may incarnate into thousands more before the planet ends. In human terms, these past and future lives could be thought of as siblings because they all spring from the same parent greaterbeing.

In actuality, the Ultimate Source is but the indirect creator of humans; it is the particular greaterbeing who is responsible for a person's existence. It is that greaterbeing who should be contacted for guidance and assistance in life.

The innerbeing is a projection from a spiritual being, it **is** the greaterbeing that created it. It is much like the fingers projecting from your hand. If you wiggle your index finger, you can feel the tension in the muscles needed to make that finger move. Your brain is concentrating on that finger to the point that it pretty much ignores the rest of the fingers, and it probably ignores the hand itself. That's the way a greaterbeing is with an innerbeing.

The soul is tied to the greaterbeing, but at the same time it actually **is** the greaterbeing. When the life is over, the greaterbeing backs out so that its innerbeing part is gone from the body. The innerbeing isn't reunited with the greaterbeing because it was never separated from it. For example, if you put your finger into a hole, it's still your finger even though you can't see it. It's your finger whether it's out of sight or not.

The soul is like your finger to your body, it's an addendum to the greaterbeing, part of the whole configuration. As the body is more than the finger, so too is the greaterbeing more than just its innerbeing. In the same manner as the fingers to the hand, the innerbeing is tied directly to the spiritual greaterbeing and to the Ultimate Entity we call God.

Free will and the lifeplan

Each human is the unique creation of its individual greaterbeing who put that person on earth to accomplish a certain lifeplan. When a human being is born, it is still spiritually connected to the greaterbeing so energy and information can continue to flow between the two.

Once turned loose as a human though, it becomes much like the parent/child relationship on earth. A parent can control a child only to a certain extent, even during the time it is in the womb. And once that baby is born, it will function as a human being on its own even more separately from the parent.

From the moment of birth you begin losing control over the infant. You cannot **make** that child go to sleep when **you** want it to go to sleep. You can lay the child down, make it comfortable, and know that it's probably tired. But you cannot **make** it sleep. The infant will go to sleep when it wants to, not when you want it to sleep.

Likewise you cannot make it eat. You can set the place and encourage it to eat, and usually there will be the desired response from the child. But you cannot force it to eat, or to drink, or to sleep.

When it learns how to talk, you can't make it talk because it has the free will to refuse. And conversely you can't make the child truly shut up because if it doesn't want to be quiet, it can carry the noise on inside its brain!

Once placed on earth by the greaterbeing, it is like this child/parent relationship: with your conscious free wills you are able to choose in life whatever you wish.

But you do come in with your lifeplan etched in your innerbeing. That lifeplan contains an outline of the experiences that you are supposed to have in order to learn the results of those lessons. For the most part, your conscious minds are not aware of the lifeplan because in the process of growing up, your psychic connection to the superconscious is clouded.

But that does not mean that your lives are without guidance. Your human decision-making process is based upon the kind of person you are, and that type of person was formed by the needs of your lifeplan. To make it clearer, it might be said that lifeplan equals innerbeing equals personality; they are all linked hand-in-hand. So in life you make decisions based upon the personality given your innerbeing. Are you emotional, obstinate, logical, willing to please, driven by power, cowed by success? When you make decisions about your life, you base them upon your particular personality traits, and therefore in all likelihood you are following your lifeplan.

Free will enters more into the actual completion of the plan. Will you use your free will to listen to your intuition and accomplish all of your lessons? Or will you choose to be lazy instead and avoid the learning situations placed before you so that only 60% of the plan is achieved? Finishing a lifeplan is a laudable accomplishment, much like graduating from college after years of effort. The preferred use of free will is to learn what was called for so that bonus experiences can be enjoyed in the time remaining.

Perhaps someone came in with just a short lesson plan. What their greaterbeing wanted to learn could have been a short thing of maybe five or ten years and the person completed the plan. But if that person uses its free will to choose not to learn the intended lessons, the same assignment could take fifty years. Even if the learning is complete in thirty years, there is still plenty of time remaining in a life to assimilate additional information.

Just because the greaterbeing began with a certain plan doesn't mean that the body has to die as soon as that plan has been fulfilled. The human can keep going on to learn other things, bonus lessons from which the greaterbeing can benefit.

When a lifeplan is nearing completion, sometimes hidden talents come out from past lives. A person might suddenly become better at something. Perhaps upon turning 70 years of age a person might successfully take up ballroom dancing even though they've previously hated it.

Free will vs. lifeplan

Each time a greaterbeing creates one of us, there is a desire to learn certain things through the life. It is your human free will which enables you to avoid learning situations, or cut off the mission at any time. Run out of the house and off a high cliff and it is over, that could be the result of using your free will. That probably does not carry out the instructions that you are here for, and that mission will still be there despite your action in this life. If in your lifetime you don't experience the things your entity has sent you for, the greaterbeing's desire still remains and will be fulfilled later in another human.

You must remember that the greaterbeing does not get upset because you do not fulfill your mission in life. The entity does not punish you for not doing what it wanted you to do. **Everything** is a learning experience for the higher self, even **not** learning. **The** greaterbeing just realizes that in the next incarnation it will try harder to make the human more compatible with the learning assignment. The entity also takes a look at what this life did learn. Because of this, each life is a positive learning experience in its own way.

When you do go astray from your lifeplan, you might feel a discomfort, a roughness in your life. There will be frustration, a feeling of being lost, or perhaps a feeling of loneliness. This is because you have closed yourself off from your very best friends on the other side and are wavering from your road map of life. You can think to yourself, "I don't know why I have this discomfort", and continue on your wayward path. Your spiritual guardians may manage to place a physicality in front of you who points to the correct road. Your free will still enables you to reply, "No, I don't like that road, nope, not today thank you". And you also have the choice to find a way off of those bumps, away from the loneliness and isolation, and onto the right track planned for you.

Usually it is difficult to use free will to ignore your lifeplan because it is so ingrained in your innerbeing that it affects decisions you make in ways that you don't realize. Even if a person uses free will and innate stubbornness to constantly make the "wrong" choices in life, it is quite probable that the lifeplan reads: "Will be contrary and suffer greatly from decisions made". Usually the direction that you think you choose freely is exactly the way you were meant to go.

Humans do not exist in a vacuum. You all live in an environment with natural forces, societal organization and other humans, all of which can affect your lives and present a number of opportunities. Typically free will is exercised in choosing which of the various opportunities available will be used to learn the appropriate lessons.

You can also use your free wills to be lazy, to maintain your life at the same level instead of getting on to the things designed for you. When the opportunity to do something, to be something, or to go somewhere else repeatedly appears in your life, they are hints to get on with your learning.

A lifeplan should properly be defined in the plural: life-plan**s**. There is more than just one lesson to learn. Free will can best be exercised by getting your lifeplans completed early. For example, even with only 80% of a lifeplan accomplished, life can seem easier and more enjoyable. In a sense, this partial completion takes some pressure off. There is then free time, fun time, bonus years to become or do more than what the script had called for.

You can not find your lifeplan written down in some book on a hidden shelf. Some do stumble upon a road sign and their guardians manage to whip their head around just in time to comprehend the message. Not all are that fortunate, and even those who have a clue need further periodic guidance. Your lifeplan is inscribed in your innerbeing and your physical guardian also knows its design. Your lifeplan can be read by those who have developed the talent of reaching the spiritual side. Some psychic mediums are able to tap into the lifeplan and relate the information to you. Instead of asking a medium when you will meet that tall, dark and handsome stranger, a better question would be one about lifeplans. "What lesson did I learn by losing my job? How will this help me in my next job?"

An exciting way is to do it yourself of course. The process of self-discovery and realization is a spiritually fulfilling event. It is preferred that you all develop your own inner feelings, those mental-to-mental images sent from the other side to guide you. The psychic realm is not just for weird people. The only requirement to participate in the psychic arena is that one be a human being. The choice is to be an active part of the situation or to sit on the sidelines and be unaware of the possibilities. The Ultimate Source did create people in Its own image. Because of this you all have a need to be consciously involved in the tremendous energy circuit, to be an active participant in the growth and evolution of the universe.

Greaterbeing-brain connection

The innerbeing and its tie to the greaterbeing are complicated, so let's begin at the far end of the configuration.

Let us say for the sake of discussion that The Ultimate Source is the most phenomenal computer ever to exist, can never be exceeded, and is a thinking computer which constantly grows. Connected to the Ultimate Source are the supercomputers which we call the greaterbeings. The greaterbeings continue through the human superconscious into our subconscious and conscious minds which are extremely advanced computers themselves. We arrive in the very advanced computer we know as the human brain. Your brain digests information from that Phenomenal Computer down through the other tie-ins and into you.

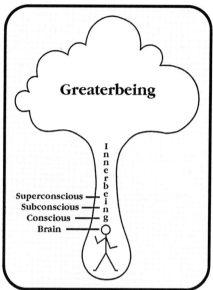

Because sleep is so important, humans have tried many experiments and experiences in terms of how long the human body physically can go without it. While asleep the energy needed to maintain the body is less, so the body uses this available energy to restore itself. It's not so much the body, but the brain which actually requires this sleeping. The brain basically needs to be "downloaded" frequently in computer terms, and that's what sleeping provides time to accomplish. The main function of sleep is to download into the subconscious all of the information stored in the brain throughout that day.

Think about all that you did today from the time that you woke up until this point now. Your brain has recorded every look, every turn of the head as you performed such tasks as getting dressed, driving your car, cleaning your house, or whatever. You don't remember all of those details but they are stored away in your brain.

The conscious brain only has a certain amount of storage available. The amount of information gathered from each day's activity is too phenomenal to store there. It would be like having a desk so cluttered that there is no room to work. A great deal of the brain's capacity is used to process all of the stimuli it receives throughout the day. That is why when you're tired, your brains behave like a full computer and tend to process more slowly, thus making your thinking more laborious and inaccurate.

The brain and the conscious state are at rest during sleep and it is at this time that their computer downloads into the subconscious. A lot of times when you sleep you're not necessarily physically tired, but really sleep deeply because the brain had a lot of information to download. Since the subconscious also has to have enough room for its processing, additional storage in the superconscious is utilized.

But the primary function of the superconscious is to send all things back and forth between the human and its entity. As minute as some things might seem, they may be important to the lifeplan. Each day is like an infinite mosaic made up of innumerable grains of sand. All of these minuscule details have to be passed to the greaterbeing. This translation through the superconscious to the greaterbeing doesn't happen instantaneously, but will all be accomplished by the time of death.

The innerbeing is not just one fluid spirit but is comprised of integers, much like the human body contains such things as the brain, internal organs, bones and muscles. In like manner, the innerbeing is made up of the conscious, the subconscious and the superconscious. Although these three elements are within the innerbeing, without the brain there is a dead end. Without the brain, there's no way of interpreting what the innerbeing is feeling. It is the brain which translates the innerbeing into words and actions through the body. It is also the brain that translates from the human condition back through the innerbeing to the greaterbeing.

The entire loop consists of the human body with its brain; then the innerbeing with its conscious, subconscious, superconscious; then the spiritual greaterbeing; and finally the Ultimate Source beyond that.

The innerbeing has possible access to information about previous existences of its greaterbeing. (The innerbeing does not have all of the greaterbeing's information because it is not equipped to handle that much data.) Any information which flows through is translated through the conscious, subconscious and superconscious of the innerbeing. These three levels of the innerbeing are the interpreters of everything back and forth between the human brain and the greaterbeing. The greaterbeing perceives in whole concepts while the innerbeing thinks in details and feelings, so there is a need for these translators.

Since most people are only aware of the conscious portion of the soul, it is understandable why they have difficulty using the other two levels to tap the information in their greaterbeings.

Conscious Mind

The conscious mind uses only part of reality, and

is what humans use to make deliberate decisions. It is the mental activity which operates when they are awake and enables them to be aware of events, situations, their own actions, and themselves as thinking beings.

Many believe that the conscious is the only thinking portion of human beings. But sometimes the subconscious will thrust a thought through the barrier into the conscious mind. The conscious mind hasn't been thinking along that line and wonders where the idea came from. Well, perhaps the subconscious has been working on it for six years! The idea can be thrown in so strongly that the conscious level almost reverberates with the idea that was formulated in the subconscious.

Subconscious Mind

The subconscious does do a lot of thinking. People have it primarily because there are things going on around the body that could be harmful. The conscious mind is inadequate for being aware of all the dangers that may be present. The mind's conscious portion does not process information fast enough to make the instantaneous decision required in an emergency. Only the subconscious is capable of that speed.

For example, you're driving down the highway and suddenly an object appears on the road. There is a whole scenario of what to do to avoid hitting that object. In the meantime you are speeding towards it and your body has yet to react. If you consciously debated all of the various possibilities of what to do, you wouldn't run out of possibilities until long after you passed over the object. But your subconscious is a supercomputer. Based upon all of its stored data, the subconscious makes your instantaneous decision. In less than a flash it translates that decision to your conscious mind so you swerve around the object, or brake, or brace for impact because it's already too late.

The conscious mind cannot be aware of everything around you, but the subconscious can. It is a very active, on-going interpreter and does most of the work in the human body. Not only does it process faster than the conscious portion, it also maintains the heartbeat, respiration, proper temperature and other basic bodily functions. The subconscious level does all of these things because it's the control room of the mind.

Dreaming

Dreaming is a very peculiar state of semiconsciousness wherein the conscious mind becomes aware of subconscious activity. Dreaming seems so unreal to the rational part of the mind because it comes from the seemingly illogical subconscious.

To visualize the dream process, imagine lots of live electrical wires with bare ends in close proximity to each other. Picture them like a swami's bed of nails, except that all of the nails are very long and flexible. Electricity is always flowing through the bed and into these nails. The nails aren't touching each other so nothing's happening. But if the nails start relaxing even more and therefore begin to sway, they accidentally touch each other during movement. When they touch, electrical sparks explode. These sparks cause more sparks. The sparks cause the nails to move away from each other. In so doing, they run into other nails and there are even more sparks. Pretty soon there are lots of sparks and lots of things happening all over.

When the brain begins to relax for sleep, all of the stored subconscious visual images, much like the electrified nails, begin to move and sway a bit. When the sparking begins, you get a collage of pictures which sometimes follow a sequence, or they can be totally irrational. These images fool the brain which keeps trying to react to these images. You feel you're a part of the sequence in which you're talking to someone, you're walking, you're singing, or being threatened, or whatever it happens to be, and then it's over. It's over because of the conscious mind's reaction to the dream.

When the conscious becomes alert, it cuts into the random movement of images and sparks. If the conscious mind becomes less alert, there is movement into the subconscious where the sparking can also fade out. It is difficult to be certain where the segments of the mind begin and end. Dreaming is a combined activity of the two elements.

<u>Dreams can seem very realistic at times, but always have a touch of unreality to them.</u> Something's just not quite right, there is an odd ingredient. Sometimes the dreamer says dumb things, or there are people who've been out of that life for years, or the person is talking to a deceased relative, or illogical comments are made. There could be a time or

dress element out of place but that's the only weird thing--the conversation seems correct but it takes place in a 1950's diner. Or everything seems natural but the attire is from the Middle Ages. Dreams also tend to be one-sided. In them things are happening to the dreamer, or the sleeper is doing something.

By contrast, astral projection is a two-sided thing where honest, original feedback of feelings or thoughts are given by another person or spirit. Everything will be of the present time period, there won't be any oddities. Any contact with the greater-being is a far more powerful spiritual experience than a dream. But we'll talk about these last two subjects later.

Sometimes the brain doesn't calm down for sleep so that downloading can take place. The brain may remain active and, for example, try to project ahead to specific scenarios for the future. A lot of times these future scenarios are based upon that day's events. The dreamer may have had something happen while driving and made a decision based upon the event. The brain settles in on that incident and plays the drama out in a different way just to see what would change. The brain wants to try a few more scenarios to see if it made the right decision during the original event.

The subconscious is generally able to function without interference from the conscious mind and is quite active in assimilating input from the total environment. The amount of information it has to work with requires even more than a computer known today. So the subconscious is a **super**computer which adds to the conscious level. In turn it's also getting input through the superconscious from the greaterbeing.

Superconscious

While the conscious and subconscious are active in their processes, the superconscious is a passive participant in the chain between the human being and the greaterbeing. The superconscious is a cushion level, a transitional stage and a data storage area instead of one that can actually take over as the other two. Although only a transitional point, it is highly effective and very important because it is the root tie and tap into the greaterbeing.

One of the functions of the superconscious is to transform the energy coming in from the greaterbeing. If the greaterbeing is 100% solid core energy, it gets broken down into two 50%'s when translating to the superconscious, which in turn breaks it down into four 25%'s into the subconscious so that it'll flow better and make it into the human. It's like translating electricity from 440 AMPS to 220 AMPS down to 110 AMPS, or from DC to AC so that the receiving instrument can utilize it.

The reason greaterbeing energy can't go directly from the superconscious to the human is because the jolt would be more than the human could handle. The greaterbeing can take direct input from the human and it can happen without translation. But this interpretation sequence through the superconscious has already been set up, so it's easier for the greaterbeing to use it too. The three levels of the innerbeing translate back and forth between the human and its greaterbeing to protect the human body.

If information transference is taking place, the superconscious translates for both the human and spiritual sides. The superconscious has to translate human information into something that the spiritual entity can work with, and vice versa. Most humans think and perceive primarily with words, detail, and emotions, whereas greaterbeings deal with entire cerebral concepts. The superconscious has to work with the information from either side and translate it for the receiving end.

You can't pinpoint the subconscious. You can't pinch off a piece and examine it. But you know it's there, and that it is the active part in human dreams. There are tests involving the conscious but they don't PROVE that it exists either, there's just an assumption that it does. There's no need to get hung up on proving the existence of the superconscious either, you just accept the fact that it exists. The superconscious and its communication ability back to the greaterbeing is just there.

Choosing the human

This complex innerbeing with its different levels comes into a certain body in a specific life situation chosen by the greaterbeing. At the time that a human body is conceived, the spiritual beings of the parents "merge" in the human sense, and send out signals as to the kind of child they would like to have. The event of conception is almost like an opening being advertised: *Human Available.*

So prior to conception, compatible spiritual

greaterbeings look at the coming human situation to determine if taking that body would be beneficial to their overall growth. The human parents are following certain paths in their lives so allied greaterbeings will begin working with the greaterbeings of the parents, getting feedback about the possible things which can be learned in life with these particular parents.

On the spiritual plane, there is only "what is". The "allied greaterbeings" doesn't refer to friends or non-friends on that side since **all greaterbeings work together**. It's based more on the path that the parents have and the future which is open for the new child. Which greaterbeing has a need to learn from a family like this? What can this third greaterbeing contribute to the parents so that they can achieve their planned goals? Thus all of the greaterbeings involved become allied in their purposes.

For example, if you were going to begin building your own house, the first thing you would need to do would be to hire a backhoe operator to dig out the dirt so the foundation could be laid. You would want to talk to people who had experience operating a backhoe. You wouldn't want to search amongst people whose only experience was nailing on a roof. That wouldn't make any sense. You're looking for "allies" in the foundation construction.

That's what happens when a new human being is begun. If the parents are financially successful, a greaterbeing that feels the need to experience poverty may not be interested in being their child. That greaterbeing may not want to go through the trouble of throwing wealth and success away in order to experience poverty. Instead, that greaterbeing may need to experience deprivation in childhood so that hurdles have to be overcome in order to be successful. That greaterbeing would not be allied with the needs of the greaterbeings who are already financially successful.

It also happens that a group of allied greaterbeings can decide beforehand which ones will project the innerbeings of the parents, which the children, which their spouses, and which the grandchildren. The decision of where and whom to be born to can happen by all manner and means.

Everyone has one

This complex innerbeing exists in every live birth of a human being because without an innerbeing the body will die. Even if that life only lasts for a few minutes, **there will be a soul** in that body. In an instance such as this, the soul will have been projected by a greaterbeing which needed to experience a short lifetime and premature death. And likewise the greaterbeings of the parents needed to experience grief due to the loss of that child.

Fetal tissue is not human until a soul has entered it. Some babies delivered with no apparent bodily functions never did have souls to sustain bodily activity. Hooking human tissue up to a magnificent medical machine to make the heart beat and the lungs expand with oxygen is not the same as a living being. If the body that is born has no soul, it **will die** no matter what attempts physicians make to establish life.

Aborted pregnancies (whether naturally spontaneous or induced) are human bodies into which no soul has entered. Abortion is a decision that gets passed on by the mother to her entity sometimes before even she is aware that it will take place. Therefore a soul never enters a fetus which is to be aborted. It is a firm, positive fact that any fetus which will be aborted either naturally, by choice, or by force will not have a soul in it.

If a baby with an innerbeing is aborted close to the natural birth, the abortion will fail and the fetus will live momentarily, a botched abortion. Birth does occur although death may follow immediately. That baby's entity needed an experience of birth and instant death.

Time of entry

Once a spiritual greaterbeing has projected a soul to take the responsibility of a certain body, it is also decided when that innerbeing will enter. The entry time depends on what experience is needed by the greaterbeings involved. Does the mother-greaterbeing need to sense the new soul living within her? Or is it something that can happen right at the end as the child is being born?

The time of soul entrance can be at any time between conception and birth that's agreed on by the greaterbeings involved. Some people are correct, at the instant of conception there are souls in some babies. But there are also some babies who do not receive souls until literally the moment of birth.

Astral projection

Once the innerbeing has entered the body, it is

not confined to being only in the body until death. Under certain conditions when the body is considered safe from harm, the soul is not fearful of projecting further than its body. Innerbeings do not have a definite shape as your bodies do--they are able to reconfigure. Astral projection is when the soul expands either out into the eons or somewhere else on earth than where its body is. It inhabits an area larger than just the body. The soul does not vacate the body because if it did, the body would die. It exists in the body and at the same time reaches out to another place much as you would reach with your arm.

At present astral projection usually happens during sleep or when the human consciousness is not interfering. It is when you **know** you've been somewhere else. But of course you couldn't have been somewhere else because your body has been right here on your own bed all of the time! Despite this, **you just know** you've had such an experience. It's so real to you because it **was** real. Memories of this astral projection are not dreams, they are more physically tangible than dreams, if conflicting terms could be used.

Occasionally during projection something may happen to startle the resting body, the soul senses that the body may be at risk, so it comes slamming back in with a sudden jerk. This results in a physical soreness for a day or two at the entry point. This area is most generally the abdomen since that is usually the site of projection. Commonly astral projection takes place without any physical aftereffects.

Astral projections can also occur when the body has been severely traumatized because the conscious mind is quite at rest in unconsciousness or coma. These are called near-death experiences and have been documented by many. The human body shows all of the signs of death, and sometimes physicians have even declared death.

A near-death experience is a superlative spiritual event realized during this time in which the person feels surrounded by immense peace emanating from a white light. Then, for no apparent medical reason, the body resumes typical life rhythms and the person returns to life. The innerbeing was never disconnected from the body during this physical trauma--if it had departed, death would have occurred and the body would not have resuscitated. Every living human being has an on-going soul in it which is necessary for that life to continue.

Walk-ins

Greaterbeings of course do have the ability to take one innerbeing out of a body while simultaneously infusing another so that the body doesn't die during the process. But realistically that wouldn't accomplish anything constructive for the greaterbeings involved--it would be more like a magic trick. The greaterbeings do not play games with you. The confusion and chaos this would create are just not worth it.

When an individual all of a sudden seems to others to become an entirely different person, it is not a parlor trick. It is something far more significant. That person suddenly has an important realization, and in so doing, instantaneously changes the direction of its life. This makes it seem like two different people, but it is indeed still the same innerbeing.

A walk-in soul appears on earth in a body at the age of 8, or 38, or 59 for instance. It's not taking over an existing body, it's just that it is here one day at whatever age. In order that it feel comfortable as a human, the walk-in has a memory of its life previous to that time, even though that history didn't actually happen. The walk-in is quite unaware of its special entrance into the world.

A walk-in can be considered an "angel of mercy" because its life is usually a short one solely for the purpose of helping others through a specific problem. They are there to help. A walk-in appears when there is a human desperately in need of guidance or protection and there is no one around adequate to provide it. They act as a bridge or stepping stone. As a human, you're out in the middle of the sea of life and you realize that there's got to be another stepping stone somewhere or you're going to figuratively drown due to your problem. You look around and suddenly there is that necessary person, that stepping stone you so desperately need.

You know walk-ins for a short time while they help you and then you never hear of them again. They're just gone. One day they walked into an earthly existence, and on another day they walked back out. The innerbeing is in as a human and after the assistance has been given, the soul returns to the ongoing entity. The body itself was created by concentrating energy. When its time is over, the energy comprising that body dissipates and the body disappears.

Animal energy forms

Every animal also has a life force which keeps their bodies alive. But that life force is not a soul as humans have. The human innerbeing is a projection from an on-going ever-developing spiritual entity, whereas an animal has merely a life-oriented energy.

The residual of the animal's energy can be distinguished in an afterlife for a while, but since there is no greaterbeing to return to, an animal's energy merges into the pool of energy called our universe. Their energy is regenerated into other animals, or converted into other energy that makes such things as the ocean's tides or the weather patterns--just as your physical bodies are.

Purposes of animals

In the beginning the object was to create humans. But in creating you, the spiritual side recognized that your environment couldn't be utterly barren. A human put into an earthly desert without water or food could not be expected to survive. There had to be an entire ecosystem into which the human bodies fit. Earthly humans could not exist on nearby planets where nitrogen is breathed because you would die. You have oxygen here because that's the way your human systems evolved. And you have animals to provide food and also be helpmates. Animals became necessary only to achieve the objective called humanity.

Some have determined that in the beginning Homo Sapiens existed as a vegetarian. Those prehistoric creatures were not as mentally astute as present day apes, nor did they live very long. Actually mankind's physical complexity does not permit it to sustain itself very well on fruits and vegetables and barks. The complexity of the human body and its brain requires the complexity of the enzymes and minerals and vitamins and everything else found in animal flesh. Therefore many kinds of animals were put here for human consumption.

Which animals you eat to maintain your bodies is a matter of choice. In other societies cats and dogs are eaten for survival, and that food is entirely acceptable to them. In your society you have domesticated these creatures as pets so eating them is unthinkable--instead you eat cows. In India cows are held in reverence and Eastern Indians do not understand how you can eat cows.

Animals should be treated with respect in the way that all living and non-living things deserve. If you treat a sheep with respect during its life, then kill it and eat it, how can that be improper? It **is** proper because otherwise sheep would be born, live and die, and then they would be nothing. Since both animals and plants have been integrated into mankind's survival mode, you should slaughter animals with respect in a way that is quickest and least offensive to both the individual human and animal. All of this is proper and the way it was intended.

Scientists are correct in their explanation of the food chain, that lower species are eaten by the upper species all the way through to mankind. There are no lions going around urging other lions not to eat the antelope the way some humans urge others not to eat animal flesh. Animal protein is not a negative, it is not inhumane to consume animals as they are a part of the necessary environment in which mankind lives.

Animals were created to service mankind. They exist for total service--not just for eating--but also to enable humans to do many things which they are not strong or fast enough to do for themselves. Animals serve these many purposes.

Over the centuries many different kinds of animals have also been domesticated at one time or another. Some unusual ones such as elephants are thought of as pets. People do not usually have elephants in their houses, but many feel towards elephants as others feel towards any pet.

Animals evolved through the system and mankind found a reason to want to domesticate these creatures. Yes, good feelings did result between the two. Although they do serve as companions, animals were not put here to alleviate the loneliness that human beings might feel--humans are available for that purpose. Human loneliness is truly corrected by getting back in touch with the spiritual greaterbeing.

Humans are the only greaterbeing-related life form. Nothing else in your universe has this special uniqueness connected to it. This fact is sad for some people who get carried away with anthropomorphizing animals into something which they are not. Animals have a brain and can communicate. They know how to function as animals, but that doesn't make them human. In a sense it is **un**natural to give your pets human qualities they do not have.

Mankind is doing the right thing in its relationship to the animals. Some humans just do not understand the entire sequence, so consequently they are misguided, but this is a learning process for them.

Contrary to many humans' fervent desires, there is no higher form of life on earth at this time than mankind, and mankind will prevail.

Animals amongst us

New kinds of creatures are constantly being evolved on earth. Recently new species of insects and spiders were noted in the United States. In the country of Viet Nam a whole series of animals were discovered that had never been known to exist before. Scientists were shocked that despite the use of chemicals in the war between Viet Nam and the United States, there was still an unscathed area where these unusual animals and insects survived.

Mankind is finding out more about its fellow earthly inhabitants all of the time. From the microorganism level to the tiny insect, right on up into the larger mammals, there are still many on this earth that have never been discovered. Birds emerging from reptiles is one of the many evolutions that have taken place along the way. They are constantly evolving just as mankind has evolved.

Whereas mankind tends to evolve more through brain development and living longer lives, animals have evolved into different species. It's as if there was a conference amongst the spiritual greaterbeings to try to enlarge the animal kingdom. Through this evolution there would be things like birds and fishes instead of just the land. The birds cause people to look up to see them. In a sense, birds are a gift because they do cause humans to look up. If you did not look up, you would soon look only down. Then you would never look into each other's eyes and pass the energy.

Whales of course are a tie to a very distant past. The whales were here at the beginning of mankind and are still with you. Mankind and the whales have been on the earth for tens of thousands of years because of adaptations to the changes in the earth. The whales have pretty much stayed whales and have passed a significant memory on through their genes. As a result, they have a substantial genetic memory of the eons back.

All of your environment is a gift, but whales are special because they feel an attraction to humankind. Whales and dolphins have highly sophisticated brains for the animals that they are. In some instances their brains are better than those of the lowest human forms of prehistoric times. Whales have a significantly higher mental capacity and feelings than many other animals. If whales could talk, they would. That's how whales have been growing in their ability to understand and attempt to communicate with humans.

There is an honest effort on those mammals' parts to communicate with humans. Their attempts are greater than those of any other species. These animals are trying to evolve to a higher level, the brain-to-brain, the mental-to-mental level to which humans are also evolving. These animals are trying to go beyond simple commands and engage in two-way communication with you. These particular animals happen to be in the water and happen to have a very high brain level. If humans expand their brain use, they will find some similarities and be able to form a kind of common mental language with the higher animals.

Many creatures have disappeared from the earth over the eons. Not all of them of course disappeared because of mankind. Some disappeared because of human folly, but others just could not adapt to the changes of everything on earth. These creatures consequently died out or mutated into other species.

If humans would stop and look, they would see that the earth is full of animal gifts. They come and they go, they're here and they grow. Some are here for brief moments while others are on earth for a much longer time. The world is a very complex system that keeps everything going and humankind thriving. It is not something that humans really have a lot of control over, even though some like to think you do.

Passing over

The only reason for a body to exist on earth is to facilitate the learning experiences of a soul and to generate energy to be shared with that soul's greaterbeing. When it is time for that life to end, the body does not die thus causing the innerbeing to leave. On the contrary, the body's death occurs because the innerbeing departs the body. Each being chooses the point where it has learned enough through a certain human incarnation and thusly decides to leave. Without the being's life force, the body collapses in death.

Close to death there is a closedown of the innerbeing in its preparation to leave. Prior to the end some innerbeings take stock. It's almost like walking through a house that you are moving out of. You walk through to make sure you've packed everything--that's the way some souls are with their bodies. They go through and make sure they've gathered all of the experience levels that they were exposed to. This can be expressed by the human in the form of reminiscing about things long past. This reminiscing also allows the innerbeing to re-enjoy its human life. Being human is pleasant for a non-physical being; soon the innerbeing will not have a physical body.

Once the soul has decided to leave the body, there's nothing to sustain that body so it dies rather rapidly. If a soul were to leave this instant, the body would be dying in its rapid fall to the floor. The soul is what keeps the body together. Without the soul there's a collapse, a nothing. Normally the innerbeing leaves at the time of death or thereafter. It happens, it's over. The instant, however long it takes, a second, a minute, an hour--just before, just after, it's just gone. The greaterbeing knows the innerbeing's time in its body is over.

The living body does have a degree of influence over just exactly when the death will occur and the soul departs. This is because of the way the body is, the way it fights passing on, the living style, the condition of the organs and all else. When it's time to pass over to the other side, the innerbeing isn't suddenly impatient to leave as it is learning something all of the time.

The innerbeing doesn't say to the human, "Let's

die now", or "Let's wait six more weeks". (That might be the message from the human to the soul though.) The greaterbeing doesn't tell the human when to die either. The greaterbeing knows when the soul's time in the body is at an end, but it doesn't declare, "Eighty-seven years, five days, six hours old--goodbye!" (If they could do that then our greaterbeings would change some other things too!) If the body suddenly makes the decision to linger three more days, for instance, the soul is right there. The body has the ability to go on, or to shorten the time, or to react. So there's a range that bodies live. The body dies when it decides to die. The body sets in motion the exact time when the innerbeing will be released. If the body suddenly makes the decision to linger three more days, for instance, the soul is right there.

The greaterbeing or its innerbeing doesn't cause the death of the body. The body ending its own life is an exception because its greater and innerbeings decided before incarnation that the lifeplan would include suicide. So yes, the higher self and the soul have decided that the body should die, but exactly when is still up to the human.

When the soul does leave, in most cases it's just at the end. The soul will stick around until the end of the body and then it's gone. Considering the numbers of human deaths that have occurred over the millennium, it's obvious that more are involved than our minds can comprehend. So there isn't this neat, easy, little clean answer about when and how the innerbeing leaves the body that will suffice for every single situation.

As the departure approaches, the energy begins to fade and the bright aura colors disappear to be replaced by the salmons, browns and black near death.

When the innerbeing passes over to the spiritual side, it's over, it's the end. It is similar to the process of reading a book. You go on chapter after chapter and finally you're at the end of the book. You don't go back and review what you've read because you remember what you've read and the way the story is tied together. The soul's greaterbeing has a perfect memory of the life lived. The greaterbeing is ready to move on to another endeavor in which it can utilize the experience gained in the life just completed.

When a soul returns to its higher self, it has to pass through what humans might recognize as a screen. Only pure, non-physical energy is capable of passing through this screen. Sometimes a soul does not realize that the body has died. Sometimes an innerbeing will refuse to leave the body behind. In cases such as these, the innerbeing will take its residual body image into the middleground with it. This residual image is not pure energy and therefore the soul cannot complete its return to the greaterbeing.

The greaterbeing is not impatient to have the innerbeing return because impatience is an earth-related time thing. If you have no boundaries of time and are eternal, how can one be impatient? What do you have to measure it against in timeless eternity?

If for some reason a greaterbeing wishes to keep moving while this soul is still in the middleground, it can expand by creating another soul into another life. However, not all innerbeings dally in the middleground, most do go directly to pure spirituality upon the death of the body.

INTO ETERNITY

We all know that the birth of a child is an important event. The parents are pleased. The siblings are excited. Relatives and friends are anxious for the birth to occur. All are awaiting the arrival of a new life into the world. Birth is the process whereby an innerbeing leaves one plane and enters another. Death is not the other side of the coin, it is the same thing. As the death of the body approaches, there is much excitement in the middleground. Souls almost line up in celebration to greet the new arrival. A human never dies alone. There is always your guardian angel in attendance. There can be your helpers there too. There can also be friends and relatives to take your spiritual hand and guide you home. Death is the birth of the innerbeing back into the spiritual realm, it is a coming home, a reunion.

An innerbeing can reach its greaterbeing in only a pure energy state. The greaterbeings to which the innerbeings return are also pure energy. If you have these billions of greaterbeings on the other side existing as pure energy, what do you have? Not **A** white light, but *massive white light**s**!* It's not a passing **through** *the White Light,* it's passing ***into*** *the White Lights*. Returning is becoming part-of once again. What those who experience near-death, and those actually passing from the earth see in this very bright light, are all of the greaterbeings on the far side.

The Middleground

Marcus

Previous descriptions of what is now called the middleground have been misunderstood by humans for centuries. One erroneous assumption is that the middleground has a physical existence.

When you read about the middleground in this chapter, you must also remember that those who populate it do not have physical forms either. Yet people they contact will describe the human form they saw. The reason for that is quite simple: if the middleground inhabitants came back to humans in their spiritual form, in their true energy form, it would continue to create the fear that we are trying to overcome.

Where does the middleground exist? Why is it populated the way it is? I assure you that as you read through this chapter, the answers are there.

As to its purpose, the middleground is a gray transitional area from the human side to the spiritual side. It is there for the understanding and the transitions needed to go from the human side back to us. It does not exist to come in from our side, but to come back from your side. It also facilitates our being in touch with humans.

4

Between Spirit and Human

	MEMBERS OF OUR UNIVERSE
Spiritual Level	The Ultimate Source
	Greaterbeings
Middleground	Instructors Guardians Helpers Learning Innerbeings Lost Souls Poltergeists
Physical Level	Human Innerbeings

Between earth and the greaterbeings on the far side there exists the vast middleground. It is just across the physical line here on earth, and is a transition zone between humanity and the greaterbeings. This haze (for lack of a better term) is a gradation from physicality to spirituality. On earth it is more physically dense and is said to appear gray. Nearest the greaterbeings there is almost no physicality and it is called the whiter side.

This middleground is where physicalness begins to end. It is only a point of reference between actual physicalness and that which is not. It can be thought of as a haze that totally envelopes the earth. The intention of this gray area is just what the name implies--a point that is nearly human and at the same time nearly spiritual. It is a point where humans could be met halfway by the many emissaries from the spiritual side.

The middleground is the superconscious of the universe. Like the superconscious of the innerbeing, the middlezone is a transitional area. Through it pass all innerbeings proceeding from a greaterbeing to their assignments on earth, all souls returning to the greaterbeing, and herein also function your guardian spirits, helpers, and instructors. The most noteworthy attribute of its residents is that they are neither purely physical nor purely spiritual, but possess qualities of each.

These souls do not exist "out there" but are rather amongst you and around you, and just beyond the point of solid physicalness in the middlezone field of energy. The middleground is wherever you are not: if you are standing where you are, and a friend is three feet away, we are everywhere in between the two of you.

The middlezone has a diverse population, but can roughly be divided into four groups called the Physical Guardians, the Helpers, the Innerbeings who have not yet returned to their greaterbeings, and the Spiritual Instructors. Innerbeings on their way to an earthly life pass through this area in less than a flash, so they are not truly residents.

Purpose of physical guardians

Every human is the unique creation of a loving greaterbeing. Each human is fashioned in order to act as the physical instrument through which the spiritual part can experience the opportunities that exist on earth. A person may not be the most creative, or the smartest, or most handsome, or tolerant or nurturing. Whatever the personality is, that exact person was carefully selected by the greaterbeing in order to fulfill the desired experience.

It is therefore important that the selected scenario be played out to its conclusion. When an innerbeing comes to earth to learn certain things for its greaterbeing, there are outside forces which can interfere with that plan by prematurely ending the human life. That would mean the greaterbeing would have to start over with a new soul to finish its plan. The guardian spirit knows exactly what that lifeplan is, and its role is to help the human avoid the unexpected that might cause the body to die or become disabled before the plan can be achieved.

There will be times when the human is concentrating so much on its human consciousness that it will ignore its natural survival instincts even though danger is present. The physical guardian is there to get the human back into a survival mode, or else to deflect the danger if necessary and possible. Some of you have felt unseen hands breaking a fall so the head doesn't hit a very deadly object. Others have sensed a protective shroud over head and shoulders while mysteriously being guided out of a burning building. These are deeds accomplished by physical guardians when danger is about to interfere with life. Sometimes a guardian just isn't able to abort the coming calamity. And sometimes a catastrophe is exactly what is called for in the lifeplan.

The length of life should not to be confused with the lifeplan. The guardian is not along necessarily to ensure that the body exists for the longest possible time. For instance, the plan may be to have a short life, and so the guardian will not interfere with that. But many are on earth for a long life to learn as much as possible. The guardian will continue protecting even after the lifeplan is complete.

Physical guardian origination

Being a physical guardian is an additional aspect of a greaterbeing's growth. The guardian is volunteered by another greaterbeing needing to learn the same lessons as the human's greaterbeing. It is much like the negotiation that occurs when a human is to be born and needs a soul. The type of life the human will live attracts a greaterbeing looking for that particular kind of education also. The kinds of things that soul will be learning--or not learning--may also apply to the volunteer greaterbeing's previous experience and future goals. So it's an alliance between your greaterbeing and another greaterbeing; one became you and the other became your guardian

Usually the guardian's greaterbeing is more experienced in human life and its dangers. This makes it a better sentry because it is aware of the many pitfalls of being human. There have been cases of very young inexperienced greaterbeings projecting a guardian spirit, and in these cases it is quite a learning event for that entity. How does one protect a human when one doesn't have much experience at being human? What is it like even being a guardian spirit?

Free will sometimes makes humans careless, especially as children. Normally the volunteer spirit has a lot of expertise to help and guide. It takes massive energy for a guardian to bump a foot to the right so it doesn't get stepped on by a horse, or to make a person change directions so it doesn't fall off a cliff. Some guardians may be extremely young, and on the other hand, others are from very old beings. These spirits volunteer to stay in the middleground working with you, guiding and protecting during your life.

Few require a lot of guardians, but some people are quite accident-prone and require up to 26 guardians to keep them safe from life's pitfalls. Each human is born with but one guardian, so those who have more receive them after birth and as needed. There are periods in life which are more stressful than others. These times require more than the average number of guardians so more are called in to assist. When life evens out again, the transient angels depart. Sometimes as death nears, a person might acquire additional guardians to help them in the transition back to the greaterbeing.

The original, main physical guardian never leaves until death since it is totally committed to its human being. Often times being a guardian is such an all-consuming responsibility that its greaterbeing will not have a human life of its own during the same period. Some people may say that their lives are very smooth and that they never have even small accidents. Perhaps this person's physical guardian is so capable that the human is never aware of the grief from which it has been saved.

Forgotten physical guardians

Communication between the human and its original guardian angel exists when the baby is born. An infant is so new and pure that it operates almost entirely on a feeling level, and so it identifies the guardian immediately. When that baby is alone with the spirit, a bond develops between the two. Small children who have not had their psychic abilities educated out of them, routinely see their guardians and play with them.

This situation doesn't last long and changes because everyone begins talking to the infant. When the baby wakes up feeling absolutely starved and begins to cry, the parent enters and starts talking to it. The little one begins to concentrate on the language and so ignores its hungry feeling. Pretty soon the child is concentrating more on the words than on its feelings.

The loss of communication with your guardians occurs because language skills are developed at the expense of inborn psychic skills. So much concentration is placed on verbal communication that the conscious mind overpowers the tie to the guardian spirit through the subconscious. Since the human no longer listens psychically, the guardian spirit has to work harder. Sometimes it even has to call in other spirits to help it get through to the "deaf" human.

As the human grows up, awareness of the guardian spirit becomes less and less. "Don't be silly, there's no play-mate in the room with you. Do you want everyone to think you're crazy?" Unless someone later mentions guardian angels, humans eventually forget what they originally knew to be true about their existence. "Do **I** have a guardian spirit?" Hopefully they start talking to it to find out if it does exist. Regardless of neglect, at least that one original guardian is still there. That guardian never leaves, it does not abandon its assignment.

There is always at least one guardian spirit for each and every human on the planet each and every minute of life, and that spirit is always the same one. Volunteered at birth, that spirit never leaves because its commitment is total. Once your greaterbeing has set your human life in motion, it assumes a passive role. All of your guardian spirits (the original and its helpers) are the active forces in your daily life. For want of a better term, guardian angels are your best friends. You and your guardian spirits are a team, **you are never alone!**

People are naturally more in tune with their guardian spirits than with the rest of the middleground. These volunteer spirits are tuned in to the correct frequencies for best communication with you. Most commonly guardian input is through the subconscious. Their point of entry is where the subconscious and superconscious blend together.

A guardian does not have the high voltage energy necessary to speak directly to you, so at times their communication comes in through the superconscious. It's almost as if your greaterbeing gives permission for the guardian's greaterbeing to come through via your superconscious. This happens at critical times when a person seems deaf, so the guardian has to go all the way back to the human's greaterbeing, then in through the superconscious to speak at a volume loud enough to be heard.

Sometimes the guardian and the human's greaterbeing use the same frequency for communication, so they may feel the same to you. Need one be concerned about where information has come from? No.

Since the greaterbeing formulated the lifeplan, and the guardian knows it and is working to see it is fulfilled, the two of them are in harmony and speak with one voice anyhow.

Helper spirits

The second group of beings in the middlezone are the helper spirits. They do not protect like the physical guardians, but function rather as business consultants, emotional comforters, or creativity enhancers for example.

These helpers assist you in discovering whatever it is that you might want to know. All kinds of information exists that can be retrieved and recreated for your particular application. The helpers sort through it all and whisper their advice into your mind.

It's almost as if all of the things known by the Ultimate Source are written individually on tiny pieces of paper that float invisibly around the cosmos, sort of like space confetti. On earth you may contemplate and ponder a solution to a problem and start searching for the answer. "Nothing in the conscious mind seems to be the answer. Okay, move into the subconscious. A blank there. All right then, how about in the superconscious? Wow, feels warmer, might be getting close to something. It's right there, if I could only put my finger on it." It feels warmer because you are now in the area where helper input is inserted. It's kind of like reaching up with a mental hand and grabbing a piece of that space confetti with a clue written upon it. There is a lot of unrelated confetti out there, and it sure does help if a spirit sorts through it first and manages to place the right tid-bit within reach!

Perhaps at work or school you are involved with a special project at which you are not particularly skilled. Helper spirits can whisper inspiration. (This book could not have been edited without the creative input of innumerable literary helpers who tossed in inspiration at every conceivable opportunity.) If one is to be very innovative, these specialized guardians could remain for the duration of a lifetime.

Only technically can helpers be considered guardians because their answers will not cause anyone harm.

Human ingenuity

This does not mean that creativity and ingenuity only come with the help of these spirits. Humans are totally capable of their own inventiveness.

An innerbeing with the capability to tap into the ultimate pool of knowledge can be born into a body which has the brain capacity for taking the leaps of faith necessary to arrive at innovation. This is like a mathematical formula. If 2+2 is 4, and 4+4 is 8--if you don't have the knowledge of 8+8, you will never get to 16. And if you don't get to 16 you won't be creative enough to extrapolate the next sequence in the line.

Yes there are previous life experiences to aid you, but humankind cannot progress if all it does is just pass on everything previously learned in the human existence. There has to be more than just a repeat of accumulated knowledge; there has to be genius on the human side to arrive at new levels. All of us together (The Ultimate Source, the greaterbeings, and humans) create what exists and will exist.

Innerbeings in transit

The third group of beings in the middlezone is comprised of human souls. These innerbeings on their way to begin an earthly life do not actually spend "time" in the middleground. For them, the middlezone is more like the highway leading to their destination. The transition from greaterbeing to human body can occur in less than a flash, and doesn't even leave an awareness of having passed through the middlezone.

After life as a human being is over, many innerbeings return to the greaterbeing in the same instantaneous fashion. For the innerbeing there is nothing stronger than its tie to return to the entity. But many innerbeings do remain for a while in the middlezone before returning to their origin.

Why innerbeings are there

Sometimes after that life of being physical is ended, there remains a tie to the earth as well as the tie to return home. Reassimilation with the greaterbeing is eventual but is not necessarily immediate. This return can occur only in a completely spiritual state of pure energy. There exists something like a screen at the furthermost side of the middlezone that prevents anything short of pure energy from passing into the spirit side. If for some reason the soul has chosen to retain anything from its life, the "screen" detains the innerbeing in the middleground.

This retention is not a punishment for anything done in life, but is rather a reminder that something is still **un**done and needs to be finished. For some it is just a natural part of the path back. Sometimes it is actually an option chosen by the innerbeing.

These souls in the middleground nearest the human side are there for numerous reasons and the following are some of the most typical.

Once the human body dies and the soul goes into the middleground, it can (but doesn't necessarily need to) pause there to evaluate with the greaterbeing what was learned, and what needs to be finished in the lifeplan. It is as if the soul says, "Look, I am who I am, but I didn't quite finish . Let me finish my life lessons by observing humans learning the same lessons". The greaterbeing considers the pro's and con's of this innerbeing continuing its work. If the life did not pick up anything it was supposed to, then many times a new life is begun right away instead. But if the innerbeing needs only the final buffing and polishing that will make it perfect, then many times the higher self permits the soul to continue in the middleground to finish its lessons. It is almost a negotiation between the greaterbeing and the innerbeing, especially for the younger spirits that want to finish in this life form rather than going back with another and starting all over again. There is still so much more for the greaterbeing to learn, the exploration of different topics if you will, that the most possible experience will be gleaned through every innerbeing.

Another soul in this middleground may need to

make some sense of its life experiences. It may need to fit the pieces together in a meaningful fashion in order to understand just exactly what it did learn. Perhaps the greaterbeing may allow the soul to figuratively sit in a rocking chair, rocking forever it seems, trying to figure out everything in its life. The greaterbeing allows the soul to sit there and rock, to contemplate, to finish the human experience, then to return home and move on.

Other souls have just not progressed toward the spiritual side and are really hung up with the human element. These souls don't want to leave and are observing the human condition back on earth. They can see the humans who have come after them and in many cases are irritated that somebody has taken over their possessions and/or territories.

There are souls in the middleground who have been there since the very beginning of humanity and haven't left yet. They may be very old in the spectrum of existence, but they are still immature. Their higher selves do not force them out because the middleground can be used for as long as the greaterbeing and innerbeing desire. A relatively short time may consist of a few hundred years. American Indians of old and Civil War personas still visit the living. Others go back for thousands of years. They are all still learning. When you are talking billions of years for a planet and eternity, then yes these spirits haven't moved on as fast, but they are learning much in the interim. A psychically aware person may catch a glimpse of one of these personas in their peripheral vision, or sense their presence. Advanced people are able to help these souls release themselves from the gray area, if the soul does desire to return to the spirit side at that time.

On the other hand, many of these middleground souls are really satisfied with where they are and what they are doing. They may have enjoyed being human so much that they really don't want to move on just yet. They can go with you to parties, explore the earth, watch their grandchildren grow up. If they did not learn much while they were alive, all of these experiences help fill in the gaps of their maturation. By observing the human condition from the middleground, souls can learn much that they did not in their own earthly lives.

There are other souls who don't realize what has happened, that their bodies have died. For a few, death may have been so unexpected that they really believe that they are still human. After a sudden death many realize that something is different, but they can not figure out what has changed. They retain a residual body image and persona and so have trapped themselves in the middleground. They continue to try to be human by remaining in a favorite house or location, remaining in the place where they died or are buried, or they might wander the earth trying to communicate with those still alive. They are lost and don't know what to do about it. Would you know what to do or where to go if all of a sudden you found yourself to be dead? There is no road sign on the other side: *Heaven 2 miles* ⇨. Sometimes these lost souls just need directions about what they are supposed to do now that they are dead, how to look for the white lights, how to get out of there and onto other things. Eventually these lost souls may realize that they have died, but continue to hang around to enjoy the middleground anyhow.

The concept of death can result in a great fear of death. Some believe that everything about themselves ends with the death of their body. Some think that upon death they will surely go to hell because they feel they have not lived up to their own standards. (Most of the time a human's belief has no effect whatsoever on what happens to its innerbeing upon passing over.) In some cases these belief systems are carried into the middleground as part of the residual body image. With this very human orientation, the soul does not recognize any of the spiritual guideposts back to the greaterbeing.

In more ways than one, you on earth are never alone. These learning souls in the middlezone can tag along everywhere you go. They are drawn to a person or family depending on the mental, emotional or physical situation they see within that group. A lover of novels may feel as though someone is reading over their shoulder or acting out the scenes--because there is a middlezone soul doing exactly that for them. Preparations for a vacation may cause more excitement on my side than yours because many of these souls love adventure. Some like to jog along through the park and throw in random thoughts as the conscious mind loosens up. There are sports enthusiasts who like to pass on final scores of the games. These souls can also interact with each other by forming their own barbershop quartet to intone the harmony they loved so much while alive. If a soul were a prankster as a human, you can assume they will be trying to scare the daylights out of some poor soul over here.

Whatever, whenever, wherever, you are never isolated because we spirits exist around and amongst all of you.

Holidays heighten awareness

There is traditionally a high level of spirit awareness during the Christmas/Chanukah holidays. This spiritual awareness has less to do with the religious holidays than one would think. It is actually due to the fewer daylight hours in the Northern Hemisphere where these holidays originated. Because of the short and gloomy days during the winter solstice, civilizations have tended to institute special holidays as focal points to make life happier during this season of darkness. (Many have concluded that Christ was actually born in the spring. Christmas was placed in December to give a reason for celebration during that dreary time.) The same thing happens on the other side of the earth at the opposite time of the year when they have their darkest hours.

Although there are artificial lights in the wintertime, there is still an overall aura of darkness. Due to the dark and cold outside, there is less opportunity to be physical. Even though you spend most of your time under artificial light, it still limits your range of activities. The result is hibernation. You obviously don't hibernate as the bears do, but in the darkened climate you spend far more time sleeping and adjusting to the lack of daylight. With not much else to do, you spend more time contemplating and thinking. (You contemplate all year of course, but not to the degree that you do when it's darkest.) You focus inwardly more when it's dark because you're inside and not distracted by the outdoors. You think about what was and the people you knew, you reminisce. All of the inwardness gets you into the subconscious, closer to the superconscious, and therefore more in touch with the innerbeings, and closer to the tap-in from the middlezone.

During this time it is easier for the souls in the middleground to communicate because you are looking inward rather than outward. These spirits want humans to tap into them. It may be that a middleground soul needs to resolve a problem with a living human, or that a human needs to settle a question with a middleground soul before it will move on to the greaterbeing. Since the spirits have more success during this season, they concentrate their efforts during the holidays. They become the center of attention and they **like** attention, that's one of the reasons they're in the middlezone. And those souls enjoying their situation in the middleground really like to talk about themselves!

Available for assistance

The best level of communication is with your physical guardians who are tuned directly to you, but these other spirits in the gray area want to communicate also. These innerbeings in the middleground and/or the helper guardians are so willing to talk that if you were really tuned into them, you would go crazy. You would hear their voices all of the time and would end up trying to pull your ears off because you could not stand all the noise. So in a way it is fortunate that these spirits do not have the frequencies to communicate easily unless you want them to.

These middleground souls can have much to offer people on earth because they have been human and have watched others be human. Assistance in whatever human endeavor can be obtained just by tuning in to this level and asking for a Helper Spirit. Human life is complicated and sometimes you can use a little extra information from such a source. In addition, there are thousands and thousands of psychic mediums able to tap into this resource for you. Information available from these middleground spirits ranges from advice on health problems, to coming possibilities in one's life, to insight for spiritual growth.

Because of their strong ties to the physical, helpful innerbeings retain much of their human egos. It is common for a psychic working with a spirit in the middlezone to begin on a good level. Unfortunately it is possible for the egos of the devotees, the medium, and/or the middleground innerbeing to cause that spirit to be thought of as a god figure. The humans involved think that the spirit has some sort of control over their lives and so begin to vie for its attention. The outcome is a cult-like situation wherein power becomes the focal point. The personality of the innerbeing becomes the attraction in lieu of its assistance. Wealth accumulation also seems to be an ingredient. As a result, the good information and the strengthening energies are sidelined.

Spiritual instructors

Since humans and the innerbeings in the middle-zone are learning, it is only natural that there be spiritual instructors. Just like teachers on earth, these non-physical beings have a great deal of experience in their field; theirs is in the spiritual advancement toward greater understanding of eternity.

Instructors exist in the gray area to help those innerbeings learn as much as they can by pointing out human interaction. And they help them to understand those lessons, since awareness does not necessarily correlate with comprehension.

The instructors are available to humans also. Amongst all of the individuals on earth interested in the psychic realm, few understand the eternal implications of it all. Many are drawn by curiosity of the unique and bizarre. They are looking, but for what they do not know. When a person reaches that point where they know what their questions are, they need instructors to provide answers.

Everyone is perfectly capable of receiving concepts through their superconscious, but that doesn't mean they can achieve it immediately. Many need to first be taught how to get to the superconscious where that communication enters. Yet others have been receiving information effortlessly since birth.

There needs to be an understanding about the difference between an innerbeing and a true instructor. As mentioned, there are many souls in the middleground ready to communicate, so one must be insistent about the level with which you want to talk. One wants to avoid communication from an innerbeing tied to the earth who will pass on opinions formulated from their human viewpoint. Request a high spiritual instructor. With the aid of these special spirits, development should accelerate.

Time for anything

The middleground itself is a level of life in which one can go back and forward in terms of earth time and life. It is as though history exists along the grooves of a phonograph record and you have the joy of going back in time or forward in time just by setting the phonograph needle down in whatever groove you choose.

Eternity is a constantly churning, spinning, fun thing. From the spirit side it is more of a continuum that goes on in a progression which does not back up. This sounds like a contradiction. How can eternity be moving forward and not moving backward when it's just been said that one can go back into the middleground in order to go backward or forward in time, or mix it all up?

For the sake of discussion, take time and put it into a bubble on the road of eternity. (Even though time is still a human measurement which does not really exist in eternity.) Since you have encapsulated all of time with its limits into this bubble, yes it can be all shaken up and rearranged. But at the same time, everything in the bubble **is** moving forward along the path of eternity.

High jinks

There are, of course, those in the middlezone

who receive most of the headlines--the poltergeists. Greaterbeings themselves do not play games with humans, but these souls do. Their psychic high jinks, as well as some of the things considered to be negative, occur only because of the ties between the middleground and humans. These pranks have nothing to do with the with the greaterbeings.

Compared to the vast numbers of souls in the middlezone, all of the pranksters combined are less than minuscule. They used to get all of the press in order to discourage humans from wanting anything to do with the middlezone at all. The characteristics of the devil were expanded to this area in hopes of keeping it off limits. But we have once again come through the Dark Ages to realize that there is a wealth of goodness and love in the middleground. We have all heard stories about souls who have come in to help some, or even to save generations of people. Not all ghost stories are scary ones, some have been quite positive.

The mischievous or malicious ones, the poltergeists, are closest to your side in terms of their physicalness. Usually they are lost on the other side, and they crave company because no one likes being lonely. Middleground spirits have no real bodies, no real voices to be heard. They do have a **flimsy residual body image** but that is not the same as the real thing. Therefore it is very difficult for a human to be aware of them under the normal conditions. For them it is rather unnerving and frightening to be in a room full of people and yet no one sees or hears them.

High jinks are perpetrated by a soul like this who is very upset about something. Sometimes the soul is upset because it did not finish what it was supposed to on earth and therefore feels it should not leave. Sometimes it is upset because while alive it used its free will instead of listening to the physical guardian. This free will choice could have led to a shortened life that did not allow enough time to finish the lifeplan. Others feel they need to help a human left behind to accept some loss or grief. These souls are frustrated and their residual humanness leads them to express it through anger. All of these conditions can result in negative feeling situations and poltergeist activity.

    Typically humans rely only on their five senses. Since you can not hear, see, smell, taste or feel a spirit, you do not believe that these souls are all around you and want to communicate. So you respond with fright instead of conversation. Some poltergeists really go awry because no one responds in the helpful way they need. Some middlegrounders are so absolutely frustrated that humans won't converse with them that they will do almost anything physical to achieve attention.

    Since they still retain some of their physicalness, it is possible for these frustrated souls to perform tricks. They are not actually mean-spirited, they are just attempting to gain attention so you will listen. They may push dishes from a shelf, slam doors, hide objects, or put things in disarray. Most of the time you react with fright or terror because of ghost stories and horror movies. There is actually no need for that since these are not monsters, just befuddled human souls.

    Because they do not have bodies, it takes an immense amount of energy for them to do anything physical. To achieve this they must gather energy from the physical world. Recalling the information about energy, when anyone draws copious energy, we say it is negative because it is the opposite of receiving energy which is a positive feeling. These mischievous spirits take lots of energy. Since it feels very negative, you erroneously call them evil demons. There are no demons and there is no hell in which to be damned. Negative energy flow does not equate with evil. A negative energy flow does get attention though. Those who ignore the energy flow certainly do take notice of objects moving around for no earthly reason. What happens if these escapades are still ignored? They escalate because the spirit is getting even more frustrated despite its best efforts to gain your attention for communication.

Normally a poltergeist just soaks up energy. It may have one of these two purposes in mind for the energy. The first is to use the energy to enhance what is left of their residual human energy. With this accomplished, when a sensitive human walks into the area it will be able to sense the strongly energized spirit. Once the human is aware of the poltergeist's presence, hopefully it will then help the soul resolve its problem. Secondly, a middlezone soul can draw the human energy around whatever it might be that it really liked while alive. It might be their favorite rocking chair, or house, or hunting ground. This makes the poltergeist feel like more of a part of the physical world and therefore more recognizable to humans.

Any of this behavior is symptomatic of the poltergeist's great frustration in not being able to gain assistance with their problem. If you truly realized what it took for that spirit to pick up that plate and throw it across the room, you would also be able to tap into communication in an instant. But you block that dialogue out of fear due to the tremendous negative feelings that accompany the energy drain and action.

Some of these souls are very powerful, and of course it takes a psychically powerful human to deal with them. The human can say, "Calm your energy and let's communicate". What appears as negativity will dissipate then because it is merely a matter of communicating. As soon as the poltergeist is told to concentrate its energy into actually interacting properly, the negative activity is usually replaced. If you have the power and strength to communicate well with them, there is nothing they can do to you. Their willpower in the middleground is not as strong as a human's. If you communicate clearly, you can talk them out of doing the things that you do not want done.

Whenever exploring the psychic, it is always possible for malicious and very negative spirits to enter the scene. Some can even lie in order to hold your attention. One can judge a spirit contact in the same way you would evaluate any human you would meet. Does it make you feel good? Does it make others feel comfortable? Does it promise unrealistic fame or wealth? You are the masters of your environment and do not have to tolerate spirits with whom you do not feel capable of dealing. Any psychic endeavor should always begin with a verbal demand that only positive helpful souls be permitted to participate.

Only those truly prepared need to try to help

these really difficult souls. Less psychically advanced humans need not get in over their heads with these fellows; just demand that they go elsewhere to save yourself a lot of turmoil. One throws a spirit out the same way you would any other undesired guest--you demand that they leave immediately and never return. Do not stop until the demand is met. Sometimes it is necessary to cease all psychic communication at that moment in order to break the link.

Many people have what they consider to be strange experiences that are actually very normal psychic events arranged by souls in the middleground. These events are usually experienced by those who do not pay particular attention to their intuition. Intuition is very important because it is communication from the middleground or the greaterbeing. If no attention is paid to this normal dialogue from the other side, bizarre situations are presented so that you will sit up and take notice. Unfortunately when humans do not understand something, they frequently become frightened and turn off all dialogue. Prayers are said and gods invoked to chase away the evil demons. You give the opposite response from the one desired! Even those who think they are intuitive but still experience odd psychic events, are ignoring some urgent message from the other side. Once the desired communication is established there will be no further need for these frightening experiences to continue.

Human vs. greaterbeing tie

Your earthly desires do not keep a Marilyn

Monroe or an Elvis Presley tied to earth. Elvis and Marilyn are long gone; their greaterbeings accomplished what they were going to accomplish. Sightings of deceased famous people are mostly mental creations of devoted fans. You have developed photographs and movies that can show what those people looked like, but they are still just inventions. This does not mean that you have "captured" their soul on film as gypsies used to believe. You have not captured their souls, you have only captured their physicalness.

The tie to the greaterbeing is strong for all of these innerbeings in the middleground. There may be an energy from the human side attempting to hold them back, but it is not as strong as that from the greaterbeing. All human innerbeings will ultimately make it back over to our side. Some will stay in the middlezone only because they want to remain. Some will stay in the physical/spiritual area for what you would call eons because the lesson they are learning is a time consuming observation lesson. They are all watching the human condition in this interim area to absorb growth for their higher beings.

Animals

Animals are a lower life species and have their own equivalency of a soul, but it is not at the same level as a human soul because it is not tied to an ongoing greaterbeing. Once they are dead, animal life forms use the middleground to regenerate into other energy forms. These include the winds, water and plants. And yes, they do come back sometimes to regenerate as other animals. Some come back and basically recycle almost like the proverbial nine lives of the cat. But most do not, many are on earth once and it is over.

Once their still-recognizable residual energy is in the middlezone, animals are able to help with those humans who have not left their body images behind. Due to their earthly familiarity, animals recycle to and from here because they are an aid in re-orienting human innerbeings. They are able to convey a calmness to these confused souls. Because of them the bewildered innerbeings are able to regain their bearings and make it back to the fully spiritual side.

Greaterbeings

Marcus

Our title "greaterbeings" does not imply that there are lesser beings anywhere along the way. Greaterbeings is only used as a term in your English to indicate the spiritual side to which you are tied. We are "greater" due to the fact that we've been around longer, because our collective knowledge is 100% of everything of every human, and because we can see through eternity.

We have the long view of eternity, and since we are in eternity, we understand it. We also understand why humans have a hard time with it. This is why some people in advanced metaphysical states step into this side to get a glimpse of eternity--to have a feeling for what we're talking about.

We grow new energy and share it with you, share your humanness and your human energy. Greaterbeings are here for the Greater Universal Good, of which every human is an eternal integral part.

5

Your Higher Self

The spiritual side is difficult to explain since most barely understand the human side of the universe. There are things on the spiritual side that are inconceivable for humans. The greaterbeings do not have emotions, do not hate, are neither male nor female, have no bodies, and do not die. Humans have all of these things and more that greaterbeings do not. Suffice it to say that we wish you to intellectualize us and think of us as the brain-to-brain connection, because in your terms we are completely cerebral.

If you were very accomplished at the brain-to-brain level, you could make a mental trip to the spiritual side and actually be with us. It would be hard to describe what we look like because in earth language there are comparatively few words for those things that you cannot see or touch. Suffice it to say that we have no physical properties to recognize.

Since greaterbeings consist only of pure energy, you would describe us as being a thinness and wispiness. If you were to put a piece of chalk sideways on a blackboard and move it down the board, you would get a wide chalk line. It would not be a sharp point, it would be a wide line of chalk with no apparent physical features. Now imagine taking that chalk off of the board and allowing it to stand on its own. Imagine further that it has the ability to move and undulate suspended thusly in space. This mental picture is similar to what an entity looks like. Even though you can look right through a greaterbeing, you would know it's there.

By visiting the us on our side, you would realize that the feeling of being here is unmatched. You would be quite happy to simply be in our company. You wouldn't feel your bodies, but you would **feel everything**, and you would **know everything**. You would also realize that it is comparable to being with your best friends. It would be an incredibly comfortable feeling. This sublime comfort stems from the fact that there are no judgments made about you. You are not criticized because of how you look, whether you are a man or a woman. You are not judged against any kind of human standards, in fact you are not judged at all. Without censure there is no reason to have fear. Think of the absolute ultimate greatest feeling you've ever had as a human--the feeling of being with us is better than that.

There is only what is

On the greaterbeing side there is no wrong and there is no right, there only is. For humans, murder is bad. For you, physical abuse is bad. On the furthermost side we do not have these human judgments. We do not make what you would call moral determinations or comments on your lives. What you do on earth is quite natural because we designed it all into your lifeplans.

On the purely spiritual side there is no time as you know it, there is only "what is". Existence here is much like being awake forever and never ever sleeping. Assume that you are awake forever and there is always light, so there are none of the traditional time measurements such as sleeping, waking, eating, working. Everything would tend to blur together if activities were not divided into sleep time, awake time, daytime, night time. Since we are purely spiritual and have no bodies, we do not notice the passage of time in these ways. Time actually is irrelevant because there is all of the time in eternity accessible to us. All of eternity is available in which "to become", to be more than what we now are.

Awareness of being

When humans sleep, you are not conscious of being asleep. When you awaken you know you have been asleep, but do not know for how long unless you check a time piece. On the physical side humans have limits of hours, days, or weeks. You use them to measure the length of time that you have been sleeping. Normally nothing happens while you are asleep as your bodies rest and your brains are at a low-active level. For this period of time you exist but are not aware of your existence on a conscious level.

Being on the spiritual side is like an on-going sleep in that there is no awareness of time. What we experience is a complete awareness of being. We exist with each other and share the knowledge and experience coming in from humans so that all of us can become more than we presently are.

Activity is cerebral

Humans have organized life by creating time and

dividing that time into segments. There are timepieces so you have a way to know how you're doing. Since spirits do not have that on this side, your first reaction is probably to exclaim: "How boring!" But consider for instance, the situation of writing a book. Think of the hours spent conceiving, writing and rewriting involved. This means no time for dancing, hiking in the mountains, nor a lot of other human activities that others like to do. How boring this would seem to anyone not interested in becoming an author. But the writer is not bored! In the same way, humans can look at the eternal existence of the spiritual level and think, "How boring", but it's not for the greaterbeings.

Imagine a stockbrokerage. There is much activity and bustling with people buying and selling. There is a great deal of energy involved in this back and forth process. But imagine the same stockbrokerage in the middle of the night when the markets are closed. There would be no humans present so it would be very quiet. The only thing remaining would be the deafening roar of the residual energy left from all of the previous buying and selling.

We are much like the stockbrokerage at night. With no bodies around, there is just a tremendously pulsating energy. When all of the activities of we spirits are put together, it would sound like a very hectic stockbrokerage room. Although all of that activity is going on, there is no feeling of being hectic, just a sense of elated being. "Being" on this side would equate to "joy" on your side. What we experience is what humans in the past have called heaven.

What we experience is not the human emotion of

joy, but that does not mean it is bland. Ours is just a different type of joy. When we say that greaterbeings are totally cerebral, that does not make us any less enjoyable. Cerebral joy can be substantial, and is more than you are capable of experiencing as humans.

If it were possible for you to visit with the spiritual entities, if you were able to tap into our energy level, about all you could perceive might be equated to hmmmmmmmmm, a hum. How horribly dull to you, but not to the greaterbeings. It's much like the air humans breathe which normally is invisible, or water which is just there--does that mean that nothing is happening on the microscopic level where you can not see? The hmmmmmmmmm is all that your ears might hear, and you would not realize that this is the sound of pure energy when it is happily at work.

On our side there is no organization that you would recognize. The entire hierarchy here is experience--not ruling, just length of being around and thus having had more experience. There is much mental cooperation entity-to-entity with no desire to compete with each other and this adds to the general aura of calmness. Here there is merely the desire to be, to grow, and to advance to the Ultimate Source.

Cooperation

In mentally visualizing the grouping and cooperation amongst greaterbeings, imagine a glass of water. Imagine us being the water in that glass. You can take a drop of water out of the glass and put it over here. You can take another drop of water out of the glass and put it over there. You can then put another teaspoonful in this spot. You can take the water all apart in this manner. But you can then scoop it all back into the glass and it is totally unified once more. If you then added a new drop of water to this existing glassful, where is the identity of that individual drop? Or if you then take one drop back out of the glass, have you taken out the drop that you just put in? Only a part of that new drop you'd just put in? Possibly. It comes out differently every time. And thus we are constantly aligning ourselves for various purposes and in so doing are different than we were before because of the new experiences.

An analogy of the greaterbeings might be your family units. When with your families it can be a very positive shared experience. Why do you do things as a family and not just as individuals? You do them as a family because you enjoy the feelings that brings. You enjoy the sharing, the moment, you enjoy everything about being in that kind of a unit. You can do all of these things by yourselves, but you like the sharing, just as we take pleasure in being with each other, and sharing with humans.

It's almost like choosing a team. One greaterbeing says "This is the goal this time on earth and here's the time frame of the human existence. Are there others interested in helping to achieve this?" And so the entities come together for that purpose. Sometimes a greaterbeing will think, "You know, there needs to be a conflict here and I'll serve as the conflict because I need to know the negativism of conflict. I could use that one this time, I need to learn that". Another one might think, "Look, why don't we try to do something where we can share the results?" This is how pacts and alliances are made.

    We of course can merge into one or ten, ten can merge into one and yet retain our own identities. And while we are merged there can be several branches together at the same time. It's almost like a Siamese relationship with two distinct entities but shared knowledge. (But it is not possible for ten greaterbeings to project one human being's soul. Each innerbeing is uniquely attached to but one greaterbeing.) Greaterbeings group together and then rearrange our energies all of the time. In very simplistic terms a spirit might say, "Well, it could be this way and maybe we ought to experience it this way". We are always creating new ideas and situations which you as human beings explore, and thereby add to your greaterbeings' overall experience package.

Endeavors

    While having a human on the physical side, a greaterbeing is consumed with the endeavor. It is not as broad based as it might be at other times because there is so much information coming in to concentrate upon. When you are alive on earth, your entity is more focused on what's happening with you in your experience, trying to guide you in the proper direction by using its total resources. This presents a conflict with the human's freedom of choice. But that's the way it is, this lack of control over the human side. It's like with your own children isn't it? You never ever thought that they would get so out of control in such a positive way.

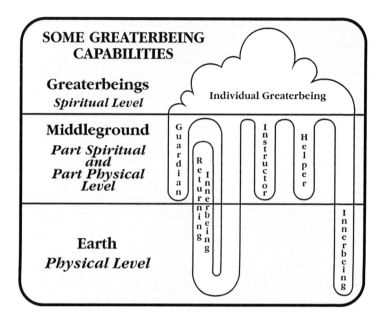

Many greaterbeings have tried extending more than one human at the same time. When a greaterbeing does have more than one incarnation at a time, they have no awareness of each other. Nor is there any personality mix-up, or any sudden personality change, or multiple personalities. These sister/brother souls are completely distinct from each other; their only connection is from each back to the common greaterbeing which does not get the two humans mixed up.

In addition to working with humans on earth, we have other endeavors. We are also dealing with the peopling and growth of other planets in the system, leaving planets that have died, leaving planets that have advanced beyond their usefulness. We are in touch with the Ultimate Source to find out where It is in Its progression and how It got there, and are passing that information on. We are sharing the experiences of earth, and preparing the attributes and plan for our the next incarnations.

On your earthly level, a greaterbeing can be involved with an innerbeing participating in existence, can have one or more souls in the middlezone, or volunteer a guardian spirit to protect another entity's human, and volunteer an instructor for the middleground.

When all of our activities are put together, it "sounds" much like that very hectic stockbrokerage room. Until humans communicate with each other in the mental-to-mental mode, it will be terribly difficult for you to conceive of this spiritual existence. Mental-to-mental is not done with words, but rather with whole concepts, ideas and desires. Your greaterbeings want to communicate with each and every one of you in this manner so that you will be able to understand us and the plan for eternity which hinges upon reincarnation.

Reincarnation

Every human innerbeing is connected to but one spiritual greaterbeing. The innerbeing is a part of that entity in the same way a branch is part of the tree. The tree needs the branch to produce leaves. The leaves are able to conduct the process of photosynthesis to provide food for the tree to keep it living and growing. Anything that is alive does grow. The leaves, branches and tree depend on each other's efforts in behalf of the whole. You and your greaterbeing are the same way, you both are indispensable to each other.

The growth via reincarnation is not something that humans do, it is something that we have to do. In the same manner as the leaves, human beings produce vital nourishment for the greaterbeing. Humans produce energy and life experiences for the greaterbeings' life and growth. It is we who mature because of our human beings.

One lifetime is but a dot along the length of eternity. A greaterbeing cannot absorb the total human experience in just one comparatively short human life. The sum knowledge that translates into the higher self as total understanding and energy growth cannot happen because of just one lifetime. This is why each of us projects many souls such as yourselves along the way; this is what has been termed reincarnation. All entities, even those just being created, have multitudes of lifetimes as humans because there is so much to be done.

A greaterbeing could be equated to a building which has to have such things as a basement, three stories, four sides, interior walls, wiring and plumbing. All of this would have to be done in order for that building to be complete. An entity is like this building. If the first human life only excavated dirt for the basement, the building (or greaterbeing) is a long way from fully complete. So it takes many lifetimes to finish that building, that entity.

A greaterbeing is a complex unit of many different ingredients, many different lives, but it is still called a singular item. If you could see an entity with all of its incarnations, it would appear to be like a cloud. A cloud is more than just a round sphere, it's full of bumps and offshoots. If you were to fly in an airplane above the cloud to view it from the other side, you would see even more lumps and bumps which comprise that whole cloud. But you don't call attention to the "multi-bumped" cloud, you just look at the whole thing and call it a cloud. By definition, a cloud is comprised of a number of areas. It's not a nice smooth thing, but it is still **one** cloud.

Likewise, a plant may have a multitude of flowers on it plus the leaves and stems and roots. We look at it also as a singular unit, and yet within that plant are these individual items. You could give each flower a different name because each flower is unique from the others. You can recognize each separate flower while still calling the whole group of them a singular plant.

The plant survives because of its roots and leaves and flowers. Winter may come along and cause the plant to hibernate deeply within its roots. When spring arrives the plant begins to grow again and puts out all new leaves and flowers. They are not the flowers that were there last summer, it is still the same plant but it has all new foliage. That doesn't negate the contribution made by the flowers of the previous summer. Last summer's flowers are not back this year, but because of them there are this summer's flowers. So too the greaterbeing survives because of its humans. Each human is different from the others, and each contributes in its own particular manner.

A returned innerbeing does not lose its identity within the scope of the entire greaterbeing either. Each one adds to the total knowledge, the total food for growth; all parts contribute to the central essence of the wholeness.

Sum total of experiences

When an entity incarnates and projects an innerbeing to the physical side, that human is tied to its one greaterbeing only, not directly to the rest of us. All of the lives the entity has experienced are tied up in the current human. This innerbeing is created out of the past existences and other endeavors that are the sum total of the greaterbeing.

It is much like making bread dough. In order to do that, you would press the dough again and again, kneading it into a silky substance. If you were to take a little part aside and fashion it into a stick of bread dough, you would have two different forms of the same dough. If you then took these two and rekneaded them into each other, you would once again have only one pile of dough. That part of the dough which was once the breadstick would be entirely mixed into the big pile once again. Even if you made another stick of dough from that big pile, it may or may not contain any of the dough from the previous breadstick. The two breadsticks you made do share a commonality. The two breadsticks have the same make-up and texture as the big pile, but each was shaped differently and pulled out differently.

When your innerbeing was put into your body, it was like taking a stick of dough from the big part and creating the smaller new innerbeing called you. What you are is a lot of the experiences from the previous lives and shared psyches of the larger mass called your greaterbeing.

YOUR HIGHER SELF

Like the breadstick, each human being is more than itself. Each one of you is the result of all of the previous lives and endeavors of your greaterbeing, plus the new experience you are living. After this life, returning to the higher self is comparable to being absorbed into a family unit. It is being reassimilated into the collective consciousness and taking part in eternity as a member of that group known as your greaterbeing as it continues through eternity.

Since a particular innerbeing or person is but a part of the whole entity, it is not the whole consciousness of that being. Together with your entity, you are greater in scope than your single existence is by itself. After meditation, many people speak of having experienced an expanded awareness, of seeming to know more than what they are capable of knowing as humans. Meditation is one method for getting in touch with one's greaterbeing, with one's total consciousness.

Humans spring from this total consciousness, from this sum of all previous lives and other endeavors of the greaterbeing. It is the whole entity which projects the next innerbeing. Will the next soul be anything like yourself? As with the breadstick, the next innerbeing may or may not be comprised of parts of yourself. It is like with siblings--some have common personality traits and some do not. Some look alike and some do not. But all siblings are part of the same unit. All share in the same family. A greaterbeing is comparable to a family. It has a variety of personalities, talents, achievements and situations. Unlike the family though, the entity has only one consciousness and each innerbeing is part of that. So in effect, each innerbeing, together with the past innerbeings and the entire makeup of the greaterbeing, decide what kind of human life will be experienced next.

Here for a lifeplan

Some people do not believe in God. Some do not talk about souls although they may unconsciously recognize that there is something in addition to the body. Some people are very religious and steeped in the historical religious customs. These are examples of your human sides and in no way reflect the overall growth level of your greaterbeing. The entity knows the spiritual level that its human is at and wants to move the person to where it will grow and realize why its life is so important.

Most people don't realize that they are tied to a greaterbeing. Some humans have no idea why you are there and what you are supposed to be doing. You just know you are supposed to be there, "there" being alive today as a human being. You seem to be lost and do not have a clue as to what you are supposed to be doing in life. You may have this feeling of confusion and do not know why you feel lost. When you look inside yourself, start developing stronger ties to the energy of your greaterbeing, start seeing auras or improving intuition, it will all become clearer.

Those of you who do not know where you are and do not know how to get in touch with the rest of your total being may not understand or accept reincarnation. Some of you may not have even heard of it. When you do learn about reincarnation, some will accept it immediately. Whichever the case, the lifeplan is at the very center of the reason for reincarnation.

If a greaterbeing is to engage in the total human experience, it cannot be done in a haphazard manner. The higher self prepares each life situation and each lifeplan carefully, because they act as the next link in the chain of growth progression.

You might be an adopted child. Or your sibling could abuse animals. Or you might live in a country rifled with political turmoil. You could possibly live in a prosperous country and eat yourself into obesity. Your ears might be too big, or you are not tall enough.

These are not necessarily accidents of birth which have to be rectified according to fickle human standards. As people, your standards for normalcy change from decade to decade and culture to culture. The woman who lines her eyelids permanently with black tattoo ink will be out of style when a more natural look returns to popularity. The woman in Africa who pierces her nose for a nose ring will not fit into German society. Who is to say what is normal and the correct way to be or look or act? Any deviation from "the norm" was selected by you and your entity. You are special. You were designed just the way you are for a reason. Your life is a situation wherein learning can take place. **We meant for your lives to be adventures in learning, not crosses to be endured.**

It is true that when life gives you lemons, you can make lemonade. That lemonade may take the form of learning to truly appreciate yourself for your individuality, or learning to cope with the bias of others because of your uniqueness, or discovering a way to bring yourself more into line with those around you. Only your lifeplan can dictate which choice will suit your needs.

Speaking simplistically, the purpose of a lifeplan is to interact with other humans so that all of us learn to advance the human condition. Because of your life here and now, your greaterbeing is advancing in wisdom. Because of your life, other humans around you advance in wisdom. The human condition advances only as all of us move together as a unit.

What small advance will be made in humankind because you are here? An advance may be made because of your act of sacrificing for others. Or you might contribute by coming in quite brilliant in order to reveal new discoveries for humankind. You might open up the psychic realm to other people so that communication with the spirit level can be more common. You all do something personal on earth, and in the long run it affects the whole of humankind. You are like a rock dropped into the middle of the ocean which causes ripples even to the edges of that great sea.

If the human condition is supposed to be advancing, how could something such as a serial killer be beneficial, especially for those who are murdered? Advances can be made due to sacrifice. Both the killer and the victims make large sacrifices by having their lives come together in such tragedy. Your communications media tend to stress these negative stories and therefore many are aware of such atrocities. Others can learn that perhaps murder is not such a desirable thing. All can learn that being such a terrible person hurts too many people. A bad thing then actually becomes a beneficial thing, and the sacrifices made are validated.

Some lifeplans are broad in scope because the design is to affect many people in the course of its unfolding. With the availability of worldwide communication and travel, it is possible today to influence a majority of the people in the world. In older eras this mobility of thoughts and bodies was not possible. By today's standards the Greek philosophers did not personally affect the thoughts of very many people. But if your thoughts can be carried forward over the generations, the effect of the Greeks has been phenomenally large in its scope.

But even if only one other human is affected by your life, that is important enough to warrant each of the days that you breathed. Even if you spent almost an entire lifetime completely alone, you were the person who learned much from that isolation.

A lifeplan can be either broad or narrow in the scope of its affect upon others. This in no way makes one lifeplan better than another.

For example, how does being the mother of two young children and dying early in their lives help the human condition at all? Because you came in to give birth to two souls who needed to develop their fortitude so that they could grow and advance due to their own efforts. It wasn't so much what you learned, but that you enabled the children to learn by your not being there.

In another instance, you live until 95 years of age. There are 75 offspring directly from you, and you affect all of their lives

Or, you find out what it is like to be totally alone because in your life nobody loves you. When you die nobody misses you and you learn how loneliness feels.

A greaterbeing is able to set up similar sounding lifeplans, and intends to learn different things from each of them. One life could be as a confidant of a politician in Roman times. Later on a life in the 1800's might be spent as the confidant of a politician in New York City. This New York life is almost a carbon copy of the life in Rome, but yet many things differ between the two. For one thing, the surrounding culture is different. The earthly time zone is changed also. Different people are met. Perhaps the influence each life has is the opposite of the other. In Rome the life was spent being Nero's friend and making him laugh. In New York the influence is more on the political level to improve conditions for people.

So what is gained by having two such similar lives? Even though they are basically duplicates with a 2,000 year time gap, different lessons are learned. The Roman life is spent as a flippant party-goer who talks Nero into doing reckless things costing many people's lives. The later life is led as a family person who is devoutly religious. Within the similarities there are several variations so that new lessons are learned.

Each life does have a purpose. That purpose may be hard to define if you apply your human standards. Your human limitations are too narrow to understand it all. But the plan makes perfect sense to the greaterbeing. You have to trust the entity which is able to see the far larger picture of eternity and how your life is beneficial. You are part of the greaterbeing and would not be placed in a situation that was not important for all of yourself.

Benefits from reincarnation

Your tie to an on-going, ever-developing greaterbeing is what separates you from the other animals on earth. The accumulation of knowledge by the on-going entity is what has enabled humans to progress beyond your fellow creatures.

Animals have learned how to fear predators and how to be alert to them, but over the generations animals have not learned how to build protective fortresses. They have not learned to stay safely within those fortresses so that predators cannot devour them. Their genetic memory makes them fear the predators, but it is not enough knowledge accumulation to enable creative solutions to the problem of safety.

It is the greaterbeings' storehouse of knowledge over many lives that enables the human brain to project the what-if's of creativity. Mankind can envision and build a fortress against the animals which could obliterate it. Humans can make a fort strong enough to thwart even the larger and stronger elephants and rhinoceroses. Mankind is also able to build a gun in order to turn the tables against any aggressive animals. (Fortunately for you, the rhinoceros has not been able to do the same thing!)

Long ago Cro-Magnon man acted about the same as the other animals due to little greaterbeing experience at being human. Each succeeding human life projected by us added to the experience pool. After a certain number of incarnations, we had experience with ideas that didn't work and those that worked better than others. Improvements could then be made upon the best ideas which would be passed to the next human incarnation. This mental evolution from generation to generation was caused by us gathering information and passing it on to succeeding humans. It is the spiritual part of you, your innerbeing, that carries this knowledge into your present life.

At the same time, the human brain was evolved so that it could translate this information into human activity. The desired result might be that fortress or gun previously mentioned.

If not for our accumulated lore, humans would not change from one generation to another--you would still be unmoved, still be in your basic mental state like the animals. Without reincarnation, mankind could never have advanced as it has done.

Breaking past-life ties

Your overall connection with your entity is complex and consists of many sections. These parts are much like the individual strands that comprise a piece of rope. You can break off some of the subconscious ties with your entity. There are many, many more wires between the human and your greaterbeing that will remain to sustain your existence.

There might be a tie from a previous life that you do not want to tolerate, such as an unexplained fear of heights. Once it has been identified as stemming from a previous incarnation instead of being learned in this life, you can break it off. That way it will not have a lingering effect and you can move on. Other times you must set in motion the desire to sever a certain tie. It is not always necessary to discover how or why that tie exists. Merely requesting that the greaterbeing dissolve it from this particular life will set that severing into motion.

As a human you do not remember every word of every conversation ever had, but the greaterbeing does, and you can tap or not tap into all areas of that knowledge. You are able to selectively forget many conversations, and yet can remember exact ones you had twenty or thirty years ago. That is selective memory. In the same manner you can "remember" ties from past lives, or elect to "dis-remember" others. So this severing of a tie can be accomplished **if** it does not interfere with your lifeplan, because sometimes a circumstance is an integral part of the lifeplan and will not be removed until the lesson is completed, if at all.

Reliving the past

Reliving a part of the earth's past may be done in order to fill a vital void in experience. For example, there could be human parents looking for a particular child to fit into their lifeplans. A greaterbeing does not want to project an innerbeing with a vital aspect missing. The greaterbeing preparing to begin life in their coming baby may have to fill an experience niche so as to be better prepared. In other words, there could be an entity for the child that would meet the expectations, but have just one little qualification missing yet.

Due to the laws of eternity, that void-filling life in the past would take place on earth. But it would not be the earth you inhabit at this time. Instead it would be the earth of the past. Within the greaterbeings exists the past earth and therefore we are able to project a human into that past. It's not done a lot, but it can be done.

You need to realize that the recreation of that past life will be over in less time than it takes to clap your hands together. The progression of eternity will not stop while greaterbeings go back to relive past human experiences. If eternity did pause for things such as this, we would never get anywhere.

Another cause for a greaterbeing revisiting the past might be at the request of its innerbeing. A soul might have the pressing desire to see a specific time period in the past. After death an innerbeing may pause in the middleground and say that it wants to experience a previous earthly time. It becomes a negotiation between it and its entity.

If the greaterbeing does agree, it brings that innerbeing back into itself and creates a new soul to experience that past. That new innerbeing and its experience in the past then become part of the total entity. The part of it that wanted this experience in the past is able to share it with the new innerbeing which actually lives the life. It is the **next** incarnation of that greaterbeing that will have the experience; the soul which wanted to see that past time will only participate in the knowledge of it.

This is a purely personal thing for that greaterbeing and its souls. No one else is involved in this endeavor. The history of the earth is replayed for that entity alone. The new soul is not there to affect the unfolding of that history, it is but an observer of the events that transpired.

It should be reemphasized that for most greaterbeings, it is not a common endeavor to go back in time because there is too much in the "future" to explore.

Greaterbeing to human tap-in

Recalling the conscious, subconscious and superconscious part of the innerbeing, it becomes evident that you have to pass through the superconscious to get into the greaterbeing. It is like the different layers of the skin. The superconscious layer is the translation level between the greaterbeing and the human. The superconscious is a cross-over zone.

The pure raw energy that comes from us would be like getting 440 amps of power into your house when you only needed 110 amps. If that happened and you plugged in a 110 toaster, that 440 would blow the appliance across the room! Quite frankly, if we appeared in front of most humans without any translation, we would scare the daylights out of you. And if you were to talk to us at our higher level, that would also scare you. So there are these levels of translation that have been developed to avoid such problems. The superconscious is like an electrical transformer or translator for your greaterbeing and you to communicate through.

At this point in your evolution, the human brain and physical capacities are lower than what is necessary for direct communication with us. If your greaterbeing filled your human body with all of its knowledge, there would be a very severe conflict. It would be almost like a constantly erupting volcano of ideas and thoughts and words so that as a human you couldn't get anything else done. If your entity exists for eternity in constant daylight without sleeping, and so kept coming directly into you twenty-four hours each day, how long would you last? It is easy to conclude that direct contact/communication with your greaterbeing would be contrary to the purpose of projecting humans. Your entity has to maintain a certain distance from you so you can concentrate only on the life you are living. You all know how dangerous it is to drive a car without paying attention. In the same manner, you must be able to pay attention to keep physically safe from premature death (and also concentrate on the here and now that is so important to your greaterbeing).

This superconscious tie to the greaterbeing becomes active when your conscious mind is more relaxed, when your consciousness is basically passed out. During this time your subconscious can work on a wider range of problems. It is at these times that your subconscious can dip down into your superconscious to touch your greaterbeing and draw upon that entity's total experience for solutions and inspiration.

With your conscious mind inactive, sleep is a good time to communicate with your entity. Do not assume that this is the only time communication can occur, because it can also happen when you are wide awake and alert. It is not just during sleep situations that entity communication occurs, because then a lot of people would say that it was just dreaming or imagination. Greaterbeing/human communication can happen at any time when the conscious mind is relaxed.

Sifting through information

Although there is a lack of conscious communication between humans and our side, your greaterbeing is concentrating on you and are aware of everything in your life. But consider the accumulated body of entities and the Energy Source on this side. And then consider that all of our endeavors are going on simultaneously. Into this mass of activity is thrown every human endeavor. This means that we have knowledge of every action and reaction, every word, every thought, every idea from the human side. All of this would have to be put into our language, looked at, analyzed, detailed and translated back into a language that you could understand before passing it back to the human side. Therefore all knowledge and all information at all times is stored within us, and answers are not necessarily readily available when humans want them.

It is difficult for all of us to speak through the few humans who can receive advanced communication from our side. Although getting all of our information back to you is terribly difficult, **it is** moving forward. We have much to say and would like to download, so to speak, from our side to all of you. Become more open to your greaterbeings. If you could all do mental-to-mental and understood concepts in a mere flash of time, we would be talking to everyone. By doing it through all of you, the few supremely advanced human interpreters would become no big deal. The drips of information now coming out would become a steady stream.

Maturation

When a greaterbeing is complete in the human realm it is basically at the highest level on the spiritual side. It is then able to spread into and grow into the other parts of the total existence. The greaterbeing continues growing and breaking and multiplying. If you look at the earth, you see the end result since its surface was formed by the inside pushing to the outside. What you see on the outside has come bubbling from the core to the surface. In like fashion we are growing to our outside edges and the new ones come from the inside.

The spiritual level is not a bland state of existence. We are a dynamic storehouse of treasures. We are a file that never forgets the actual experiences, the actuality of being and experiencing is always there to be reviewed over and over again if desired.

Through a succession of human lives such as yourselves, we add every experience and learning situation you encounter to our store-house. Each life adds a facet to its entity's character, and therefore to the rest of us.

You might think of us much like the human maturation process. You are born smooth and round. But as you grow and learn through time, your body develops wrinkles as signs of hierarchy in human experience. An experienced one of us might look like a Bear Claw pastry that has all of the knobs on it.

"Knobs" or "bumps" of experience appear on the entity after many lives. Some of us oldest greaterbeings have so many knobs of experience that they begin to blend together and appear to be almost smooth and round once more.

Tribulations

Marcus

Many of you wonder why your life is not perfect. Your definition of what would be a perfect life is usually from a self-centered position based on acquisition of material well-being. That of course, is very human.

Your overall reason for being is to share the energy and add to the universal collective knowledge of which you are a part.

We must get that knowledge somehow, so there are lives that many humans will say are less than perfect. They involve unnatural death, disease, unhappiness, physical problems, mental problems. They involve having excessive wealth. They involve having excessive happiness. Your earthly lives involve the entire spectrum of what the human mind can conceive.

Others may look at your life and say they wish they had it. You may realize that your life is not perfect and wish you had somebody else's. But after reading this you will realize that you are on your life path. You should be congratulated for succeeding because that lifeplan is why you are there.

6

Life Can Be Difficult

The Ultimate Source and the greaterbeings continue to generate and grow because of experience. The universe will also go on and develop for millenniums yet. It is like the ever-pushing wildflowers that keep multiplying in the fields. Everything is on a tremendous growth spiral. This growth is partially due to the entity experience on earth. All aspects of your human condition--the good, the sad, the success, the failure, exuberance and depression, are valuable when viewed as a whole. All things learned build a stronger entity just as life experiences build a stronger human being. Human suffering is but a portion of the total picture, but one which concerns you on the human side.

Human condition

The human condition is better today than it was 10,000 years ago. That may seem odd to some who hear this, until one realizes that 10,000 years in the evolution of eternity is no big deal. There have been a lot of recent changes made, particularly in the United States. Generally speaking, Americans do not fear that someone will purposefully and maliciously do them physical harm the way others do in lesser developed societies. You are free to move about in life regardless of the position into which you are born.

You do not have to concern yourselves with such things as collecting water for household use each day. People in the slums of the United States live far better than the peasants in most Third World countries. The worst in this country is better off than the worst is elsewhere. Compared to what it once was, the human condition has moved up dramatically as a whole throughout most of the world. This upward spiral will continue as it is part of the upward movement of creation.

Many of you consider yourselves to be enduring unbearable hardships in your lives. You feel this way because you do not realize the greater suffering endured by previous incarnations of your entity. When your greaterbeing puts a new innerbeing into a body on earth, it knows the level to which previous bodies have suffered. The entity has endured experiences throughout human history, and in its perspective, yours is not suffering when compared to the others. For example, greater suffering was probably endured by a young black slave who had her feet broken by her master as punishment. Her misconduct was that she had run to the adjoining plantation to visit her mother.

Autistic children, the blind, deformed, deaf and apparently witless humans throughout the world are looked upon with pity. Many of these souls came in under those conditions to observe and learn in silence. It's an incredibly painful way to live of course, but they do observe. Yes their human bodies suffer, but you have to take into consideration what their souls are absorbing. They are from very young entities--and old ones too--who just have not experienced those conditions. These humans are like sponges--even the blind can see, even the deaf hear, as that is the miracle of the souls.

Pacts for experience

There are millions and millions of greaterbeings who have not yet experienced all of the various modes of human heartbreak. In order to facilitate the forward movement of so many souls at one time, we sometimes come into the world in large groups to experience the same difficulty. All wars of the past-- the Hundred Year's War, the Crusades, World Wars I and II--are examples of this kind of unbelievable suffering.

Many of those born from 1892-1925 were in a group of souls who came in to certain areas of the world (Japan, the United States, Germany and Italy) having common lifeplans for negativity. These children of the nineteen-tens, twenties and thirties were serving the purpose of their entities. Some were from young greaterbeings needing to learn some of the negative things of war. Of course there are always old entities mixed in. "Young" and "old" are relative in our language and have nothing to do with the comprehension of human experience.

Many inexperienced souls came in as a big group wanting to know what they would learn from World War II. A vast majority of them unfortunately are stuck now in the middleground because they do not understand that what they learned is just what they learned, and that now they need to apply it. In the middleground they are still trying to figure out how to apply what they learned: suffering and being without. They did not learn much happiness--they pretended to be happy but they were not all that happy. Some are growing and changing, and some are not.

Disease

Due to the dissolution of the Soviet Union in the early 1990's, the superpower political tension between it and the United States evaporated. This resulted in a world-wide sigh of relief because the strong possibility of war on a huge scale appeared to go with it. You would have had another war sooner or later without the fall of Communism and the decline of Americanism. There would have been a war involving multitudes of peoples. Due to the mass destructive capabilities of these super-powers, sides would have been taken by other countries as a protective measure. A great deal of suffering would have ensued. The nuclear threat from these two countries actually was obliterated from your near future.

As a further result of this, disease is now replacing human war and conflict. Those greaterbeings still needing to go through human physical misery are now suffering at their own hands. Absolute misery and suffering is now centered on the African continent. There is greater affliction going on in Central Africa than there is being endured in the rest of the world combined--including countries like India, Bangladesh, China and Indonesia.

Multitudes of souls are dumping into Africa in order to quickly learn about suffering and dying. It is a short ordeal of suffering. Many of these souls coming in are young. They have formed another pact, a big group of them to come together and endure the disease called AIDS. There is not a war to suffer, so they experience this incredible disease, starvation and famine in Africa.

The world is beginning to look at Africa and realize that AIDS needs to be controlled or else it will spread into the entire human condition. Within the next few years there will suddenly be a recognition that Africa will explode if there is not genuine and sincere help given by the world to contain disease in that area. This acknowledgment will lead to massive research to ease pressure there and begin to end the suffering.

AIDS will not become the all-inclusive world devastating disease that some people fear. It will not be as devastating as the Black Plague of the Middle Ages which almost wiped out Western civilization. In the next few years it will become possible for AIDS to be controlled with medication. It will always remain serious for humans, but in time will be controllable and not wreak the havoc of which it is capable.

Human commonality

The human cause for this great African suffering has been racial bigotry. White people in particular look upon Africa as the sewer of humanity. As a result, not much has been done to help those people. It has been easier to deal with the Latins and Asians, the fairer-skinned peoples. This superiority attitude goes back three or four hundred years to the days of slavery and is taking a long time to work its way out of the human psyche. At this point racism in the United States is just kind of there and being muffled. The inattention to Africa's problems is the residual effect of this racial hatred.

But humanity is beginning to realize that white, black, yellow, you are actually all the same. Leaders try to make each group appear to be different from everyone else, but the ones you see in the communications media are not the people you run into in everyday life. All of you suffer from the same problems and concerns and blemishes. You are not different from each other, you are just portrayed that way. The media will soon realize the negativity of their reporting, they will see that it is not positive to report the news that way. You are all growing to a oneness of peoples, wherein the color of the skin will mean nothing of importance.

All experience is positive

On our side we do not make judgments about your human lives, as there is no sin. Sexual preference is a part of your human condition and it also has its place in greaterbeing education. Despite this fact, there are going to be people prejudiced against homosexuality. These people feel that if they accept homosexuality, that they will have to accept pedophiles. If they accept that, then they feel they would have to accept the idea that it is okay to go on a killing rampage.

Since homosexuality is a part of the human condition, a better reaction is to acknowledge--not necessarily accept--that things like homosexuality exist as part of your situation.

Acknowledgment does not necessitate one's participation. Being a homosexual, bank robber, rapist, bigamist, child abuser, or any topic chosen, does not affect the soul's ability to learn and pass information back and forth to its greaterbeing; it is not a negative thing. Muggers also have a soul in them which does mature from their venture.

Humans who draw prejudicial conclusions about others are in an exploration mode. "What happens if I do this? Is there any resistance to it? Does it come back? What happens if I do that?" People are tall, people are short, have differently colored skin, disabilities, no disabilities, are homo or heterosexual. It is everybody pushing and trying these different things.

People without prejudice have backgrounds wherein the differences are not important. These people say, "Well, you know, it just is". And they move on because they do not have time to worry about pushing anymore. A lot of humans have not advanced to this point. If you were all one color, one language and one height, it would give those people who are pushing other's buttons far less to push on, and they would have to move on to the more important tasks of growing and developing.

Karma

The course of eternity is to progress, and therefore the traditional concept of bad--or even good karma--does not fit into the picture. There can be no retribution or reward for deeds in another lifetime. If that were the case, then humans would never advance because you would always be settling past scores.

All humans have suffered somehow at the hands of others. If in Life #1 you suffered at the hands of Another's Life #1, karma would indicate that in Life #2 you make Another's Life #2 suffer, and in Life #3 the other makes you suffer. At this rate there would never be any forward movement.

That concept of Karma is an oversimplification of the greaterbeing's need to experience the whole spectrum. Just because a someone has experienced one end of a range, there isn't automatic knowledge of what the opposite circumstance is like. An entity may opt in one lifetime to be a power**ful** prison guard and in another to be power**less** as a rape victim. These balancing situations may not even be casted with the same other greaterbeing involved.

Where great grievous human injury has resulted at the hands of one to another, many times it is totally forgotten in the next life or even the next several lives. You may never again encounter that reincarnation that injured you. If you do, you may feel negativity upon meeting that other human being. You will not know why you do not like that person, so you will be wary of them. That is usually all that results from unpleasant past life experiences.

Any experiences from past lives brought into this one are only through the greaterbeing's choice in order to cause further learning in the new situation. Because lifetimes of suffering and inflicting suffering are freely chosen, there is no one else responsible for the situation and therefore no retribution is needed.

Lifeplan interference

There are people who have the need to be

around those in pain, and who feel the need to help those who are in distress. For instance, there are people who truly believe that everybody should be required to learn sign language so that deaf people are never left out of conversation. Another example might be, "We know what poverty is like, so let's end it for these others". These people are learning the frustrations of trying to implement something that they sincerely believe. They are learning how hard it is to get another person to learn from their experience. Just because they have suffered does not mean that others can tap into their feelings and realize what suffering is all about.

Some people are actively trying to abolish the death penalty. If a soul wants to come down to do something that humans think is improper, such as murder for example, then that soul knows it could be punished. That soul wants to learn the aspects of murder. Being the victim the next time may be the plan so that the greaterbeing can learn both sides. The plan could even be to learn what it is like to kill and then be killed for that act, all in the same lifetime. If the execution is discontinued, that soul has not learned all that it intended to learn from the experience, and the lifeplan has been thwarted.

No one is able to pass judgment upon another's situation. There are many who would not believe they were suffering even if they were told that they were. A child in Cleveland, Ohio, probably believes that everyone else in the whole world is hot and uncomfortable in the summer. When that youngster lies in bed on an August night, it believes children all over the globe are sweating too. This is not considered as suffering by that child, it's just the way life is for everyone. But the person in Denver, Colorado, with its cool night breezes wonders why anyone would continue to suffer through Cleveland's hot and humid summers. The Cleveland child does not consider itself to be suffering--and isn't that child the better judge of what it experiences?

So suffering is relative; what is suffering for one is not necessarily suffering for another. For instance, there are some who believe that everyone in the gutter is in dire circumstances. If someone in the gutter raises a hand and says, "Help me", you help them. But you cannot be all knowing, all-understanding, wonderfully meddlesome human beings and look at somebody in the gutter and exclaim, "You poor soul, I'll help you out of this". Helping one out of the gutter who does not want out may be interfering with that soul's lifeplan; being helpful and productive might actually be counterproductive for the soul in the gutter.

There are homeless people who do not feel that they are suffering. These people look around and reply, "I don't have a mortgage payment, I don't have pressures, I'm eating, I'm comfortable, and I know who I am". They are satisfied with the way they are. Humans must be careful about how they define suffering. It is not necessarily bad nor undesirable to the one experiencing the situation.

We travel together

The learning that takes place in your earthly existence is comparable to a long line of rafts floating down a river. The passengers in these rafts are all of humanity. Each of your rafts is tied to the one in front of it and the one behind it so that the rafts cannot be separated. We are all tied together on our journey on the river of eternity. If the last raft gets hung up on something and cannot proceed, then neither can any of the others because we are all tied together in this progression.

People in the first raft round a corner of the river and have knowledge about that point, they are are further advanced than those in the rear. Those in the last raft are not as advanced only because they have not yet reached that point in the river. All will travel down the same river, all will ultimately pass the same points on the river, and all will ultimately gain the same knowledge and advancement.

Suppose there are two people sitting in the last raft, and one accidentally slips and hits the other. The one who got hit reactively slaps the other who slaps back as its reflex action. Up ahead in the lead raft, souls have more experience than these two. When the same thing happens, the one who slips immediately says to the other, "I'm sorry, I slipped and hit you". The reply is, "No problem, it was an accident. It's okay, it didn't really hurt".

You are all together, some of you have just learned more about hitting, about making others suffer, and about your own suffering. Yet it is important to explain this to those in the rearmost rafts. They probably will not understand it until they reach that point in the river where they can see what you are talking about. Until that point, acknowledgment of their level of maturation is the key.

Future level

Even the physical suffering unfolding in Africa now is truly far better than it was only five thousand years ago. In our future, humans will be the beneficiaries of the forward movement of the human condition from your point to theirs. In your future, humans will look back and think that you are suffering compared to their advanced situation at that time.

The method of suffering will also change in your future. It will be endured less as large groups of people, and tend to be experienced more on an individual level through personal tribulations and problems. There is much to be learned through paralysis, loss of senses, mental illness and deformities. This type of anguish will continue until the need to learn from all of that will be over and the greaterbeing level will move on.

Mental-to-mental

As humanity continues into the future and advances into the psychic, into the mental-to-mental, other things will change along with it. In the future people will be able to routinely pass entire concepts to each other via their brain waves. At that time there will be no need for words or paragraphs to be spoken or read; the entire experience will be passed from mind to mind in an instant. It is much like the times now when something is said or done and two bystanders look each other in the eyes and realize that they have the same thoughts.

Because of their lack of physical superiority,

women and smaller men have been dominated by larger males. As humans evolve mentally, females and the physically meek will finally turn the tables. Their mental levels will be able to compete one-on-one with the physical brutes. There will be more equity than was ever possible in the physical sense. In the mental-to-mental time, suffering will be less on a physical level and more on the mental.

In the future, those who choose to suffer will not be capable of the mental-to-mental interaction. A statement of pity at that time might be: "Isn't it a shame that Tom here can only talk!" People who can only speak and are unable to get through on the mental-to-mental level, will in the future be looked upon as being different. They will be viewed much as a deaf person is today who needs special help because they cannot hear.

Since we have always functioned with mental-to-mental communication, one might conclude that it would be necessary for one of each type of life to be lived, and then the entities could share that knowledge and avoid duplication. But it is still like humans relating experiences to each other. You can listen to the description of how another took an ice cream cone and plopped it against their forehead. Your fingers could be pressed against the other's skin in order to feel the residual cold from the ice cream, and you would still not know the exact sensation of the experience. You would still lack the direct knowledge of that feeling. You would want to do it for yourself.

If it were possible to pass direct knowledge, humans could do every conceivable thing just once. That knowledge would pass to the greaterbeing involved and it would be shared with all of the others. Although that knowledge receipt by the others still results in the reception of energy for the energy circuit, it is still not like getting as much as when you do it yourself. In order to gain the full benefit of each experience, the greaterbeings need to have them directly, as well as share them indirectly.

If new greaterbeings are always being created, will they all have to go on repeating the same experiences? Will we ever really progress then? Fortunately there is an intelligent design to all of this. A new entity grows out of, emerges from, spins off from another, and is at the same time an equal to it. Therefore, new ones do have direct knowledge of what has been experienced by the entity from which they proceeded.

Perhaps it is time to take a closer look at how all of this is structured.

The Ultimate Source

Marcus

There came to be the existence of energy and in its growth there was a knowing and understanding.

The Ultimate Source recognized by looking in a different direction, that others were around and sharing and growing from the energy. That is how what you now determine to be the spiritual side, occurred. At the point it started, there was forever. We have been around forever. From that point to now seems as short for us as your earthly lives feel to you.

During that time we began to understand what eternity and forever meant. In earth terms, we went for millions of years before there was a plan to create beings--not just earthlings, but beings.

The Ultimate Source is a leader for all beings. We cannot make that word any more simple than it is--all beings. Do not read into that word only humans. But do not concern yourself with how many others there might be and what they look like.

Do not concern yourself with the topic of other

beings. You are part of us, you will see when you come back from your current existence where we all are and where we are going. Accept that knowledge then as your reward for a job well done as a human.

For now accept the challenges you face in going beyond this book into the next level of advancement. The human energy generated by your growth is very important to universal energy.

The Ultimate Source continues to be the roots and trunk and branches of the spiritual side. The Ultimate Source is so covered with this continual growth of everyone that if you were to look, you would not be able to discern between It (which has been forever) and all of us (who will be forever also)

7
God and Us

On earth you are captives of time, that measurement which tells you where you are in the passing of your days. You measure almost everything with time. When should I be there? How old are you? How long have you lived there? How many minutes until dinner?

There is no time element on the spiritual plane, so in essence it could be said that there is "time" for everything because eternity will not be ending. Eternity extends further into the future than you could possibly run, shoot a bullet, or send a photon at the speed of light. As humans you cannot comprehend how far into the future eternity extends. Because you cannot comprehend the absence of time or the length of eternity, it is also impossible for you to understand the beginning of eternity. It is hard to conceive of eternity having a beginning, but it did.

Ultimate Source begins eternity

There were particles of energy which existed. They drifted and drifted until as chance would have it, they came together, and from that grew The Ultimate Source. Of course the immediate question is "Where did the material come from for The Ultimate Source?"

The spontaneous combustion of The Ultimate Source into that which is, is incomprehensible for the human mind at its present level. If it were understandable, you would have the answer to one of your oldest questions. Suffice it to say that It was just there and feeding on itself--almost a spontaneous combustion situation of a bright nothing. There was this starting point just occurring and The Ultimate Being came out of it. The Original Being came together, it began. The ability and knowledge basically clicked on. In the human sense, The Ultimate Source began because It looked around, It just turn-ed around and saw that It was. With that was a knowledge, and with that knowledge was eternity.

Ultimate Source replicates

The Source turned around again within that knowledge and wisdom of having been, and in this turning again there were other entities. The Source realized It had within It the ability--the unconscious ability--to reproduce, to spin off. It was more of an unconscious act which It realized It had the ability to do. This replication just occurred and it was not really important to understand how, there were not any questions by The Original Source. It was as if The Ultimate Source had said, "If I am, they can be!" And others were. We were just there. The numbers do not matter because that is a human invention; but we would be talking tens rather than millions. Do not get the impression that there was a multitude suddenly. It just grew over a span of "time" amongst this eternity.

These new greaterbeings were not quite as

knowledgeable because they were not quite as old; they were eternity less some amount from The Ultimate Source. As It created these new equals minus what you would call the time and experience differential, it is important to realize that we were equals. We were not like newborns that had to grow and mature--It created equals to Itself. We had not been as long as God, and therefore were infinity less a short amount. But in all other regards we were/are equals.

As equals we existed and worked together. After our creation we grew to the level of where The Ultimate Source had been, and learned the things that It knew. We could ultimately turn around and there were more of us. Again, this was not massive in numbers, it was a learning, a passing on of the knowledge of how to. It was not as though we learned to reproduce, it all just grew to that level.

Creating the cosmos

Out of all of this also grew the ultimate infinite spheres and explosions that became the universes that spread out to fill the vast void. Since the explosion spawned everything, all of the universes are approximately the same age. Your scientists have been trying to appoint the time when it all started and how it all came to be. It was rather near the earth that this explosion took place, and the earth caught the eyes (if there were eyes) of us all. The planet earth is bright in intensity, and it was bright and cheery at that time also.

Since that moment the planet earth has continued

to change, and is so complex that man has yet to figure out the very basics. Scientists are going off in this direction when they should be going in that direction, but they do not realize that yet.

The earth is going to do what the earth wants because the immense energy used to create it has never left and continues to dominate its purpose. The earth's energy to be what it is can only be equalled by the combined energies of each and every human channeled in the same direction at the same time. Anything less than that total commitment and the energy of the earth remains stronger than you humans. You can get together and cause comparatively lesser cataclysmic events such as wars, famines, droughts--but these only affect the earth's energy to a minor degree. It is much easier for humans to affect each other by war and such because they are human-on-human. It is difficult for you to affect the earth's will to be what it is.

Creativity was not enough

Creating the physicalness of the universes was an awesome event. Upon observing the explosion which had created the cosmos, we remarked "Look what we did, look how we did it!"

Although we had all created what was, something wasn't quite right. We looked around and said in effect, "We're missing some**thing** about ourselves". We knew what we had done by creating the cosmos, but We lacked the physicalness to appreciate the result of our actions. The level that we were at was almost like being stuck in the mud and we needed to get out. We realized the level of energy that we were and had, but knew it was not the ultimate maximum level of which we were capable. Of course we could stay at that lower level, but we knew that it was not enough. There had to be something more.

In the vernacular sense, we were essentially bored. "Well, if we're going to be here forever and this is the middle of forever, what are we going to do now?" And The Source said, "We are going to grow and develop and move on". And we asked, "How are we going to do that?" And It said, "That's a good question. We have all of these worlds out there, why don't we do something with them?" And our reply was, "That's great, let's do something with them! What should we do?"

Solution is physical

The solution to our dilemma was much like the elements of oxygen and hydrogen. Separately oxygen and hydrogen are valuable and identifiable, together they are water. Together the two are more than they were individually. They do not need the other to exist, but they do need each other to be water. Our side needed your physical side in order to become more. In order to do anything with our physical creation, we needed a physical presence within it that would be a compound of our spiritualness and the physicality of the universe.

To make a long story short, after much discussion on how to handle this whole dilemma (and billions of us do discuss things) humans were created. It would have been so easy if it were done the way it was related in the Bible: On this day God made the world, and then on this day God made the humans, and everything went happily thereafter. God Itself did not have the recipe.

We all created humans together. We needed a physical presence in the cosmos in order to fill our void with physical experiences provided by human beings. But we realized that we could not put you physical beings into a sterile environment--that wouldn't provide enough learning experiences. So all sorts of plant and animal life forms were created in order to provide a stimulating environment for you.

Sharing without regeneration

Creation was a make-it-up-as-you-go-along scenario. In the beginning of the earth we needed to make adjustments in the energy level to overcome the mistakes. And after we created humans we learned we had drained ourselves in the whole process.

Our energy was at a very low level and had to climb back up despite the fact that prehistoric humans could not contribute much to the energy pool. For one thing, we did not know how to communicate with the human levels we had formed--try spiritual communication with one of those basic creatures not much brighter than the animals around them!

Going back to the time of Christ and several generations before that, it was extremely difficult to communicate with human beings. The energy sharing problem prompted us to think perhaps we had made a mistake by having the human side at all. When you were created, we did not realize that we would lose contact with you.

Regeneration now building

On the eternal scale, 100 million years ago is as yesterday. On the infinity scale it was not very long ago that it all began, therefore much progress has actually been made. Immense strides have been made in getting the energy level back up to where it should be. Through trial and error we learned to spiral ourselves up to a point and then let the human energy level build and spiral up to meet us. Then we spiral up again and your human energy level catches up once more. We lead and you follow. We did not know how to do that in the beginning. So it has been all of these millions of years to get to this point where we are today. We are now at the point where humans are able to understand the complexity of your tie-in to us and The Ultimate Source. This comprehension on your side now enables **all** components of the energy circuit to combine our resources toward the common goals created by The Original Being.

When energy sharing (communication) occurs now between the spiritual and physical planes, we are elated because the energy exchange enables us all to grow faster. With this energy we can propel into the future of humanity at an ever-increasing speed. On your side you see it as technology, scientific breakthrough and advancement. This is all the result of the higher energy level finally getting momentum. This higher energy feeds on itself. We are able to advance our learning plans more rapidly because you are now able to understand what the design is and how you contribute to it.

Ultimate Being shares with all

Even though The Ultimate Source is more distant from you on earth than we are, It is an integral part of your existence. The Original Entity does not appear before you and say, "I am The Ultimate Source and I'm responsible for all of this!" That is a fantasy that humans have invented--God sitting on His throne watching billions and billions of acts of worship. When the Christian Bible was penned it was written that "God created Man in His image". So one human looked at the other and concluded, "That's what you look like, therefore God must be an older one of us since He's wiser". It is your invention that God is just this super-equal human. You find it hard to think of The Ultimate Source as an energy vapor, so you think of It in your human sense. God is not offended if you do not think of It as a vapor and a super-intelligence.

Because of the ties through us down to humans, there is an ever-expanding growth in understanding and development on all levels which then passes back to the Ultimate Source. One could say that The Ultimate Being is therefore on an ever-increasing spiritual high because of all of us.

You realize the joy a human feels when its child has done something on its own and is beaming with pride in itself. The child has done something great which the parent also thinks is incredible. The parent experiences a joy that is an incredible inner glow even though it had nothing directly to do with the child's accomplishment. The parent looks at it all and thinks it is very good, and that fills it with this inner glow and joy.

GOD AND US

That is basically what The Ultimate Source is doing because of creation. It's joy in you is enjoyed and shared with all of us. The Ultimate Source is pulsating Its energy through us to the middlezone and to you. This strong energy pulsating all of the way from The Ultimate Being may seem weak when it gets down to your level, but at full original strength, it would propel you completely out of the universe!

This pulsating energy is a combination of that great inner glow caused by the things that The Ultimate Source has created, plus the growth that is continually taking place in all of creation. All of us are constantly forging into new territories of knowledge and experience; together we are an eternally dynamic force.

This high level of energy results in a very **positive** feeling for The Original Being. It is comparable to having inner goosebumps, to having warm fuzzies when somebody does something good for you. The Ultimate Source's experience of you is kind of like one of those all of the time; you are a pulsating good feeling for It.

And remember, it is that two-way circuit again, it's not all just going to The Ultimate Source who takes it all in and is selfish. It is still a circuit. It does go to the Ultimate Being, but after taking the energy in, It charges it up to be something stronger than it was, and then whips it back through to those of us in the rest of the circuit. This regeneration of that energy back through to humans is a good feeling for The Ultimate Source. Being more God-like simply means learning to unselfishly share this energy with the rest of creation.

We Love to Communicate

Marcus

As You read Jean Ann's comments, realize that she had to leave what she considered to be a normal family-oriented life, and tell the world that what is in this book is true because she heard it first-hand. By putting her name to this book and sharing this information with you, she has made a real change both in herself and others.

She knows there's humor on this side and wants to share with everybody the wonderful feeling that she's had over all the years in gathering this information.

Read her words, they are reassuring. And remember, through JeanAnn, through Tom, and through you, there is more information to be learned. We are always around, and as JeanAnn says, we even have a sense of humor.

9
Epilogue

By JeanAnn Fitzgerald

During a trance session while nearing the completion of this book, the speaking greaterbeing suggested that I write the last chapter. The thought crossed my mind that they might be joking, but then they never joked about serious matters. That is not to say that greaterbeings are humorless, that the spiritual side is only serious. They've explained that they have extremely cerebral humor, and that they can make jokes which humans understand.

This playfulness was exhibited many times. Once during a trance session I brought up the subject of how the spiritual and physical planes seemed to be at opposites. I remarked that it was kind of like the typical male-female relationship, and that it was no wonder we had trouble communicating and understanding each other from the physical to the spiritual plane. The following is a trance excerpt from that session.

JeanAnn - *"It seems strange to be at the point where you think you understand greaterbeings and The Ultimate Source, about how pure and pulsating and everything, how non-verbal and unemotional you are. And then to wonder how you created this world with all of its emotions and flaws, Created it down to the little bugs and specks of dirt, the minute detail that there is, when you seem to be at the opposite end of the spectrum and so unrelated to us."*

Greaterbeing - "More related than you realize."

JeanAnn - "I'm sure. But as greaterbeings you don't have eyes, you don't have ears, you don't have emotions, you don't have hates. We on the other hand have all of these things."

Greaterbeing - "We don't have bodies."

JeanAnn - "And you don't have bodies and we have bodies. You don't die, we do die."

Greaterbeing - "The real you doesn't die either."

JeanAnn - "Our bodies, you know I meant our bodies die. We have right and wrong while you don't make judgments. We have our brains..."

Greaterbeing - "Never been told we didn't have any brains! "

At the precise instant this comment came zipping in, I knew it was not said because they had taken offense, but because they were indeed kidding me! I realized that because at the same time I experienced a tremendous love.

One thing I have always marvelled about was their never-wavering understanding of us. As human beings we mostly experience love with strings attached. It is an indescribable event to be the recipient of the unconditional love that they exude. That unconditional love remains no matter what we might do or say. All humans are loved, understood, and are appreciated for who we are.

The greaterbeings have prescribed four or five more of these informational books which will entail

EPILOGUE

discussion in greater depth plus new subject matter. I do look forward to the times I will spend with these incredible beings during Tom's future trance work.

They have already channeled many hours of conversation through Tom. Each trance session necessitates several hours of transcription and information cataloging. It was tedious to prepare it for this book. One day while organizing the haphazard information into a human kind of sequence, I realized that they had answered for me one of the basic questions of all time.

Ever since humankind evolved to the point that it could comprehend its own beginning and end, or the process of cause and effect, there has existed the query: Why am I here? The question is older than the written history of the human race.

The early Greek mathematician and philosopher Pythagoras felt that the human soul was imprisoned in the body and condemned to a cycle of reincarnation due to the fall from its original state of bliss. For the most part, that disfavor idea parallels the Judeo-Christian concept which followed 600 years later: the doctrine of Original Sin which resulted in Adam and Eve being cast out of the Garden of Paradise. (Rumors abound that the Bible once contained references to reincarnation but that they have been necessarily deleted over the years.)

The Hindu doctrine of Yoga also mentions that the soul is a stranger to the world of physical matter into which, for unknown reasons, it has fallen and become enslaved. This belief system teaches that through meditation, deliverance from bondage can be obtained by dissociation from the physical world and detachment from objects which bring pleasure (there is that sin idea again). Even many Western philosophers believed that the soul is not in its proper place in this evil world, that it is a stranger imprisoned in the physical body.

I can understand that last part about being a stranger in this physical presence of mine that I see in the mirror, and in these hands as I write these words. It is that feeling of not quite being all here in the physical plane. For me that has always been merely another sign of the existence of the spiritual innerbeing and the rest of our existence beyond that.

Unlike the aforementioned philosophers, I have never viewed being human as a curse. Punishment as the purpose for being here seemed to be quite unproductive. A God such as this seemed to be contradictory and self-defeating. Why would an All-Knowing God not realize that less-than omniscient humans would probably fail any test He prescribed? Why would God create beings in His image just to punish them through all of these eons? Religion never seemed to make much sense when I checked it against what I felt through my innerbeing.

We have tended to answer the question of existence from our human perspective: that mankind is the center of the universe and that all can be explained only from our viewpoint. In the Seventeenth Century it was too much of a shock to humanity's fragile ego to consider that the planet it inhabited was not the center of the universe and the object around which all else congregated. The Catholic Church excommunicated Galileo for concluding scientifically that the earth revolved around the sun. Without his improved telescope, it was difficult to realize that the earth is not the center of our planetary system.

And now this channeled greaterbeing information presents a complete enough picture from which to draw a valid concept about the spiritual side of our universe. Human life is not at the center of creation--the greaterbeings are. When we look at it with their perspective, things make more sense. Being here is not a punishment for us. Being alive is a mission, it's a joyous adventure we are able to fulfill with our entities. Our existence is a completion of the energy circuit. Without humanity's earthly experiences and generation of energy, The Ultimate Source and the greaterbeings (and therefore even ourselves) could not continue their rapid growth spiral. Without us they would stagnate. Without the lessons we learn by our interaction with each other and the energy we produce by being alive, nothing could be dramatically more than it presently is.

You Are, and Therefore I Love You

You're the reason I can walk on the earth,
And relish all the pleasure of breathing.
I can smile as my eyes greet the sunshine,
And see all the things that we're being.

I stride forward in adventures of existence
Full of confidence I will find great reward.
'Tho I falter I will master and enjoy
Everyone of the days that we soared.

You are the being that I need for fulfillment
Of my potential, my weak points, my yearnings.
It is you who can teach me to be
All I strive for and know we'll be learning.

Your shortcomings are fodder for growth
As by contrast I know where we'll be.
And your triumphs are reasons for medals
As we rise to the levels we see.

You're my doing, I am you, we are one,
You are the instrument and I the melody.
I'm your greaterbeing, the one who has formed you,
Who glories in the fact that you're me.

YOU ARE, AND THEREFORE I LOVE YOU

Earth humans are creatures who tend
To have standards and values that are based
On success at whatever is current
While the true worth is ignored, left to waste.

What others may perceive as your person
Is only what's noticed in haste.
Look instead at your soul that is inside
And realize that you're not commonplace.

We were born long ago before earth time
Making us older than Methuselah or your star sun,
More beautiful than Diana or David,
And wiser than owls or King Solomon.

Do not look in the mirror for your image,
For those are mere atoms and light rays.
Look at me to see the reflection
Of your greatness and the reason I say

If I'd wanted another I'd have done so,
But you're the center of perfection I chose
For your goodness, your flaws and ability
To live and enable us to grow.

My Dearest, remember I love you,
And if no other can see what we be,
Come nestle in the arms of my love force
And shout to the rooftops, you're me!

JeanAnn Fitzgerald

Channeler's Comments

By Tom Fitzgerald

While exploring events in the psychic realm with some friends in 1977, I allowed myself to trance channel for the first time. As we were all being initiated into this type of venture, we did not realize that some people in trance should not be physically touched by another person without permission. Because there is such a massive amount of energy required from the other side to accomplish the event, the touch acts as a shortcircuit interrupting the energy flow. This shortcircuit causes the energy to become concentrated at the point of contact. Since my wife did touch me, I therefore bore the red imprint of her fingertips on the side of my body for several days thereafter.

Despite the shock of her touch we continued with the trance. During that first session we helped a lost soul in the middleground to pass back to the white lights. It was such a gratifying experience that we continued trancing for the next six years, ever mindful that I shouldn't be physically touched. Almost immediately, entity instructors were the prime spirits who spoke through me. They provided much elementary information about how God, the Ultimate Source, had structured eternity. But because of my innate skepticism of the whole idea of the psychic, plus the pressures of daily living, I allowed my logical human side to interrupt my psychic progress for several years thereafter.

INTO ETERNITY

My interest in communicating with the other side was rekindled because of a reading I received from a medium in 1992. She strongly warned me that if I did not immediately resume trance work and write a book, I would become very sick for ignoring my entity's planned work for me in this life. You have to realize that it is tedious for me to write a good business letter, let alone a whole book. Besides, what would I write about?

So despite some skepticism, I began channeling again. This time there was a difference in the information. There was a definite air of seriousness. Immediately there were instructions furnished as to what I should be doing in my lifeplan (spreading the information about the Ultimate Source and eternity) and how it would all come together for my public speaking on the subject. Because of my doubts, our instructors caused several personal things in my life to change for the better. These changes convinced me to follow their outline. I began to realize that I really did have the ability to communicate with the other side for the benefit of all.

A final step to assuage my misgivings was when the instructors took me across the expanse to the spiritual side in order to experience them firsthand at their level. I was able to "see" them in my mind's eye. In order to "see" a spirit entity, imagine a piece of chalk placed flat against a blackboard. If the chalk is moved down the blackboard, you get a wide chalk line -- not a sharp point, but a wide line, a kind of thinness and wispiness. If you then visualize taking that chalk -- only the chalk -- off of the blackboard and letting it stand on its own, it would not fall. It would kind of move and undulate in space. An entity is like the chalk, it does not have features. Do not imagine a face or a body. Because you see it in your mind, there are no looks and you learn how unimportant features are. Even though you can look right through an entity, you **know** it is there.

The feeling while being with the entities is unmatched. A very comfortable feeling equal to being with one you love very deeply. There is absolutely no fear--it is not spooky. These are your best friends and you are happy to be in that state with them. There is no pain. You do not feel something like we do now with our bodies. But you do **feel** everything, you **know** everything. You know when you "see" them on that side rather than just feeling them from this side. You are not judged by how you look, whether you are a man or woman, young or old. You are not judged at all. There are no judgments about you or your life. It feels so great, it transcends, it **exceeds** any other feeling I have ever had as a human. Imagine the absolute greatest feeling you have ever had--being with them is better.

But then, just who are these "greaterbeings"? Who are these entities who felt it so important for you to be exposed to their information that they worked very hard to get me to this point? Lots of humans channel communication from the spiritual plane, so what's so special about this? In the beginning there was just the Ultimate Source. The first beings spun off from this Original Being were the spiritual entities; from The Ultimate Source and the entities were then produced the cosmos, all of the souls in the middle-ground, and all of us human beings. These spiritual entities passing the information in this book are co-equals with the Ultimate Source. Most psychic mediums receive information only from souls in the middleground who are these entities' creations. The information in this book is from those nearest The Original Source. They've asked me to use the term "psychic interpreter" so as not to be confused with the more traditional psychic mediums. I am not the only psychic interpreter in the world today, but the others are not prepared to assume the role of teacher also. It evidently is up to me to teach others that the psychic realm is a positive area that all of us need to understand.

I began to think about some of the psychic comments I had heard over the years. Some of it was said by people who suddenly knew intuitively that a loved one was dead. "I just **knew** it happened. It wasn't that my brain reached a logical conclusion, the knowledge that I **knew** was not logical--I could see the whole thing happening in a flash, it was instant knowledge." Unfortunately, it often takes a dire situation such as that to be powerful enough to knock down the barriers so our subconscious can receive information from the other side. This does not make intuition bad or spooky or the work of the devil. Nor does this person **make** that event happen. Lots of good, positive information will be received by everyone once there are no barriers.

Most people have had positive psychic experiences but didn't know that was what they were. Perhaps they had seen auras, that excess energy just dripping off of everyone of us. Or maybe their souls had astral projected to another place. A lot of people never mention these experiences to others. They think they are the only person to ever have anything strange like that happen to them. They keep these events tightly locked up in their minds and so never realize that many others have had them also.

Even scientists have had many experiences in the psychic. Despite this, some of them still ask, "So what proof is there that the spiritual level exists?" Because they can take some hydrogen and mix it with oxygen to create water, they are trying to prove the existence of the spiritual realm in the same way. That is like taking sonar into space to locate schools of fish--they are using the wrong equipment. They try to dismiss it all by saying, "Well, that's my brain". **That is just what the goal is!** We are trying to get the brain to that level. Instead, the scientists should go "Yes-- we've achieved the brain level! What they need to realize is that without their innerbeing, they would not be. They ought to look more at their being. They ought to look at the strength of their brain. They ought to know that when they get these alleged intuitive ideas, the 'CALL HOME' messages from loved ones, that there is something greater than the human body and that we have no machines at this time to measure and thus cannot provide their concrete proof. The psychic is not concrete, it is not physical as we know it.

And still people say, 'Well, how do I know that this isn't just Tom talking? How do I know this is right?" The answer is that **you** must make the decision. You've made decisions in the past. With this decision, you may not know why, but you **know** it's right, you **feel** it's right. Everybody can identify with that, when you **feel** it's right. I can't explain it. Trust me, I **know** it's right. They feel it. You feel it. That is where we are on this. Those who get into communication and open it up with the spiritual side will make the awareness grow. That's the answer. It seems simplistic perhaps, but why does it have to be complicated?

Today there are many people practicing psychic awareness because they have been in touch with their entities and their guardian spirits. One of these people may be your best friend who has never spoken about it yet. Or it may be yourself. There are now more people than ever before who understand and can communicate what is happening on the other side. There is such peace and calm amongst so many people who practice this; we have people who are reading everything they can on this subject and they feel it is the right way to go; we can look at the serenity level of so many people who **want** to participate. It crosses all classes, ages, gender and cultural barriers. There has to be something to it.

Along with the firsthand experience of the entity level that I described, I also had quite a bit of information acquired from our instructor/interpreter entities in my trance sessions. They revealed that all of the data they were passing on through me was to be the heart of the book we were to write for all those people looking for knowledge about their side. Each session took the form of a wandering casual conversation between the spiritual entities who spoke collectively through one entity spokesperson through me to my wife. It became her task to sort, collate and prepare the information so that it would read well for you.

CHANNELER'S COMMENTS

This book is a natural way for us to convey this information. If the spiritual entities from the other side could appear to convince us that this is all correct, they would have to look like humans. If they didn't look like humans, you would probably be afraid and not want to believe. It is generally believed that something must be evil or suspect if the messenger doesn't look like a normal human. Therefore, this information is being passed on in the more conventional manner of this book so you can evaluate it freely at your own pace.

Some of my family members and friends are taken aback by our endeavor since they are steeped in traditional religious attitudes. They fear that anything along psychic lines is part of the occult and that the devil is involved. If you believe there is a devil, if you believe that God is a punishing god and these are truly your functioning beliefs at this time, then you are correct in not participating in psychic events or sharing your psychic experiences with others. There is not an easy way to convince you that this is the normal human condition. What you need to do is check your inner self, check with your innerbeing and follow the religious beliefs that you have. Question your religious beliefs to the level that you desire to question them. One of two things will happen: Your strength in your religious beliefs will grow; or you will start to run into other people who share your religious point of view but are not as afraid of the psychic level. These people will be able to communicate with you about the psychic realm. If you are then more comfortable with the psychic realm, come on back. If this doesn't happen, do **not** be upset that it didn't happen. Do not condemn others who are communicating differently than you by being involved in the psychic arena.

All of this knowledge about us and them, about how things truly are, was revealed by a body of entities. By speaking as a group, they wanted to lend credence to the fact that they are all in accord concerning this information, that it isn't just the idea of one entity or person. What we received was the result of a collectiveness of the entities. On their side of the barrier between the human and non-human, there is more of a collecting of the energies and a sharing of their knowledge. It is more collective so that when we tapped into it, practically every time a different entity was the spokesperson passing on their combined words. It wasn't one entity speaking to us, it was all of them putting it into words to communicate; the spokesperson was merely the interpreter for their collectivism. Entities were coming through in a random pattern, all with the same continuous flow of information on the same topics and to the same depth. By speaking as a group, their goal was to make the psychic realm better understood for what it is. Without the interference of a distinct personality giving the information, you can concentrate on the content instead of on who provided it.

The entities began the endeavor of channeling this book, this encyclopedia of communication of what truly is, in order to cause an historic change in we humans. This change will be more significant and lasting than any previous to it. This change, they said, will come to fruition long after we are all gone, but these words will be the basis for humanity's change in thought. These words are the foundation for spreading eternal love, teaching us how to unlock the eternal love in all of us so we can share it with the entirety of creation. This change will be positive because we are now ready and have the need to be positive--it will be a win/win situation for all of us; it is their gift to mankind.

Those who are ready to participate in the next level of this eternal journey will appreciate this book. Those who are skeptical will seek more proof. Those who do not believe will cast critical comments and fear. Nonetheless, all of you will have the opportunity to actively participate in the great adventure which is planned for our future in eternity.

Reno, Nevada
Spring, 1993

About the Channeler

A leading businessman and active community leader for many years, Tom was apprehensive about selling his business and devoting full time to the metaphysical pursuits of channeling, healing, writing, radio and television programs and personal readings.

He was pleasantly surprsed when the main reaction was summed up with: "You read minds? But how can you, you're so normal looking!"

That's why Tom is in such demand as a teacher, speaker, and counselor. People attend his classes and seminars because the information he shares is presented in a manner consistent with integrating metaphysics into daily living for everyday people.

Contact Tom to arrange individual or group presentations and life/health readings at:

Phone: 702/828-7194
Internet: http://www.energycircuit.com
Email: tom@marcus.reno.nv.us

About the Editor

Having dabbled in writing all her life, editing this book afforded JeanAnn the chance to hone her skills. Upon completion of *Into Eternity*, she decided to express the book's concepts in story form, showing how they worked in the average individual's life. The result is *Angelheart, a Metaphysical Story of Love*.

Numerological revelations about one's purpose on earth led her to combine that metaphysical discipline with handwriting analysis. The result was a psychic reading that explains people's lives through numerology, then their handwriting reveals which attitude and belief modifications will make that life more enjoyable.

JeanAnn may be contacted for a handwriting-numerology reading at:

Phone: 702/828-7194
Internet: http://www.energycircuit.com
Email: jeanann@marcus.reno.nv.us